Making a Real Difference with Diversity

A Guide to Institutional Change

*By Alma R. Clayton-Pedersen, Sharon Parker,
Daryl G. Smith, José F. Moreno, and
Daniel Hiroyuki Teraguchi*

Nancy O'Neill, Contributing Editor

Association
of American
Colleges and
Universities

1818 R Street, NW, Washington, DC 20009

Copyright © 2007 by the Association of American Colleges and Universities.
All rights reserved.

ISBN 978-0-9779210-5-8

To order additional copies of this publication, or to learn about other AAC&U publications, visit www.aacu.org, e-mail pub_desk@aacu.org, or call 202.387.3760.

The work on which this monograph was based, as well as the publication itself, was supported by a grant from the James Irvine Foundation.

Contents

About the Publication v

Acknowledgments vii

Introduction 1

Chapter 1: The Journey from "Project-itis" to Coordinated Action 9

Chapter 2: Quantitative Findings 19

Chapter 3: Qualitative Findings 25

Chapter 4: Promising Practices 45

Chapter 5: A Guide to Comprehensive Diversity Work 61

Conclusion 71

References 77

Appendix 1: Campus Strategies by Dimension 81

Appendix 2: CDI Evaluation Project Institutionalization Rubric 83

Appendix 3: Summary of *Guidelines for Creating an Evaluation Plan* 91

Appendix 4: Summary of *CDI Evaluation Project Resource Kit* 95

About the Authors 97

About the Publication

This publication is drawn from the work of the James Irvine Foundation Campus Diversity Initiative (CDI). The foundation established the CDI, a $29 million effort, to assist twenty-eight independent colleges and universities in California with strategically improving campus diversity. The six-year initiative (2000–2005) supported a range of activities and institutional changes with the aim of increasing access and success of low-income and underrepresented minority students in higher education.

The CDI included a strong evaluation component to help each institution focus its strategies and track institutional goals. A team of researchers from Claremont Graduate University and the Association of American Colleges and Universities (AAC&U) designed and led the CDI Evaluation Project to assist the CDI campuses in developing their own evaluation expertise and mechanisms. A larger evaluation resource team (ERT) worked with participating campuses to measure success, make mid-course corrections, and ultimately broaden and sustain diversity efforts beyond the scope and phase of the grant-funded projects.

Another purpose of the CDI Evaluation Project was to contribute new knowledge about effective diversity practices to the higher education field. In addition to this monograph, the project issued three research briefs, an impact study, and a resource kit. More information can be found at www.aacu.org/irvinediveval or www.irvine.org/publications/by_topic/education.shtml.

CDI Colleges and Universities
California Institute of Technology, California Lutheran University, California College of Arts, Claremont Graduate University, Claremont McKenna College, Dominican University of California, Fresno Pacific University, Harvey Mudd College, Holy Names College, Loyola Marymount University, Mills College, Mount Saint Mary's College, Notre Dame de Namur University (formerly College of Notre Dame), Occidental College, Pepperdine University, Pitzer College, Pomona College, Santa Clara University, Scripps College, St. Mary's College of California, Stanford University, University of La Verne, University of the Pacific, University of Redlands, University of San Francisco, University of Southern California, Westmont College, and Whittier College

Evaluation Resource Team
Suzanne Benally, Campus Liaison; Susan E. Borrego, Campus Liaison; Jocelyn Chong, Research Associate; Alma R. Clayton-Pedersen, Co-principal Investigator; Mari Luna De La Rosa, Research Associate; Mildred García, Campus Liaison; Jennie Spencer Green, Campus Liaison; José F. Moreno, Senior Research Analyst; Sharon Parker, Co-principal Investigator; Daryl G. Smith, Co-principal Investigator; Daniel Hiroyuki Teraguchi, Research Associate; Belinda Vea, Research Associate

Acknowledgments

We thank James E. Canales, president and CEO of the James Irvine Foundation, for his commitment to and support of the CDI and the CDI Evaluation Project, and Martha S. Campbell, vice president for programs, for her leadership throughout the initiative. We also thank Robert Shireman, Rosa L. Armendáriz, and Hilda Hernández-Gravelle for their important work in conceptualizing and launching the CDI.

We are grateful to the staff at the Claremont Graduate University School of Educational Studies and to Siah Annand and Misha Charles at AAC&U for their dedicated assistance with the project, and we are also grateful to past and present evaluation resource team (ERT) members for their invaluable contributions to this work. Special thanks go to the campus liaisons, whose insights helped shape the work of the campuses and the content of this monograph. Specifically, Susan E. Borrego, vice president for student affairs at California State University, Monterey Bay, brought to the project expertise in student and academic affairs collaborations, service-learning projects, leadership development, and community outreach. Suzanne Benally, associate vice president for academic affairs and chief diversity officer at Naropa University, contributed her knowledge of American Indian education and of methods to increase minority participation in higher education at both the undergraduate and graduate levels. Mildred García, president of Berkeley College, New York and New Jersey, enriched our work by sharing her expertise in diversity and institutional change, faculty development, and mentoring underrepresented students, faculty, staff, and administrators. Likewise, Jennie Spencer Green, professor in residence at Loyola Marymount University, brought to the work her expertise in multilingual education, organizational change, and urban education.

We thank Nancy O'Neill for her extraordinary work as contributing editor of this monograph. Nancy also served as editor for the impact study and the three research briefs that were published as part of the CDI Evaluation Project. She has been extremely skilled in framing the vision of the project as well as the study findings for multiple audiences. She has a deep understanding of diversity issues in a campus context, and we are grateful for her contributions to both the form and content of this work.

We also thank additional staff at AAC&U, especially Shelley Johnson Carey, Michael Ferguson, and Darbi Bossman in the office of communication and public affairs and Nakia Bell in the office of education and institutional renewal, for their work on this publication.

Finally, none of this would have been possible without the dedicated efforts of a great many individuals on the CDI campuses. We thank them for undertaking the very important work of improving college access and success for underserved students and for their willingness to move along a path toward organizational learning. We have learned a great deal from their experiences, and we are pleased to be able to share some of lessons we have derived from them with the broader higher education community.

Introduction

A New Vision for Diversity in the Twenty-first Century

Contrary to the popular conceptions of higher education as a staid, tradition-bound entity removed from the vagaries of the world, changes in the academy over the last five decades have been stunning. If someone were to compare the recent profile of almost any college or university to its profile in the mid-twentieth century, the contrast would be striking. Instead of de jure segregation, one would find racial/ethnic diversity that has increased to the point where, nationally, nearly one-third of the student body is comprised of students of color. Instead of having students who are almost exclusively from the upper class attending college, today 75 percent of students who graduate from high school eventually spend some time in higher education. A once overwhelmingly male college-going population has given way to a female majority on many campuses. Where college attendance was once synonymous with the experience of eighteen- to twenty-two-year-olds, today 40 percent of students are older than twenty-two. Religious quotas have been replaced by an increasingly varied spectrum of faith commitments and communities. And the perceivable changes go on and on.

Demographic changes are less pronounced among administrators and faculty, but today's campus leadership is nonetheless dramatically different from that of the 1950s. Important new content areas and modes of inquiry have also expanded the traditional disciplines and resulted in stunning new interdisciplinary fields. The practice of studying only a very narrow swath of human history has given way to examining all of human civilization—not just in Europe or the United States, but across the globe. And the "ivory tower" that once cloistered students from neighboring communities has gradually given way to more overtures of partnerships that, in some cases, have turned the world beyond the tower into a classroom.

This democratic progress did not just happen because fifty years had passed. It occurred because of national legislation, allocation of funds, student protests, civil rights and other social movements, and presidential executive orders. It occurred, too, because of the actions of courageous faculty, visionary administrators, concerned students, and determined student affairs personnel. And the changes became part of the system because people came to believe the academy was a better place for them.

While one can chart trajectories of progress over time, some dilemmas remain unresolved and progress itself can produce new dilemmas that require new solutions. One dilemma involves the persistent achievement gap faced by many students of color and low-income students, as well as a tendency among higher education leaders to want to "fix" these students—usually by sending a small group to remedial programs—rather than focus on the institutional structures, policies, and practices that hinder so many.

Another dilemma involves the serious lag in diversifying the faculty, staff, administrative, and trustee ranks in higher education, even on campuses with significant compositional diversity among students.[1] Faculty members, especially, play a critical role in the education, research, and service functions of the academy, from teaching and learning to knowledge development to university governance. Campus leaders today have begun to recognize that to truly achieve excellence in all of these areas, they must tap the kind of intellectual power and innovation that comes from a professoriate that is diverse in terms of race/ethnicity, gender, class, religion, and other social identity dimensions. Furthermore, given recent arguments to the Supreme Court that stress the importance of such diversity to the mission of higher education, faculty diversity—or the lack thereof—serves as an indicator of the academy's continuing societal legitimacy.

A third dilemma is a lack of comprehensive systems for evaluation and assessment on many college campuses. While this is not specific to issues of diversity, lack of evaluation mechanisms affect this work when campuses are unable to demonstrate the positive impact that diversity, however it is defined, can have on student learning, organizational culture, curriculum reform, scholarship across the disciplines, campus–community relations, and other critical areas of campus life. The lack of evaluation mechanisms also hinders an institution's ability to determine if and where there is progress in achieving its goals for diversity. Without the proper systems in place for evaluation and assessment, institutions risk the expenditure of resources on programs and practices that may not work, but—due to conventional wisdom or to a need for quick "solutions"—are nonetheless launched.

A fourth dilemma facing those involved in diversity work in higher education today relates to questions of definition and practice. In some cases, diversity has multiple and seemingly endless definitions, and many college and university leaders bypass serious engagement with the meanings held by various campus constituents. In other cases, diversity is equated with the composition of the student body, typically the racial/ethnic or gender composition. This important but narrow focus excludes concerns about the composition of other constituent groups on campus, as well as important concerns about how different constituents perceive and interact with the institutional environment. This narrow focus also excludes questions about how diversity plays out in curriculum and scholarship, the status of equity in access to educational opportunities and achievement of important learning outcomes, and many other areas.

Equally important is the need for serious and sustained attention to how campuses *do* diversity work—an issue that lies at the heart of this monograph. Decades of diversity efforts have proven that narrow vision and isolated action will yield only limited results. Most campuses today have some set of initiatives designed to enhance compositional diversity, create more inclusive communities, or expand intellectual horizons. Yet few have the coordinating structures and evaluation processes necessary

---

1 Compositional diversity here is defined as the numerical and proportional racial/ethnic composition of an organization's members (Milem, Dey, and White 2004). For this monograph, the members include the student body, faculty, administration, staff, and board of trustees of a campus.

for these endeavors to have a broader and more powerful impact on the institution and on student learning and achievement.

The complexities of the twenty-first century require a fundamental shift in how the higher education community envisions campus diversity work. This shift is both conceptual and practical, and it centers on moving from narrow constructs and piecemeal approaches to coherent, intentional, and comprehensive thought and action. Conceptually, diversity must move from being thought of as the responsibility of a few designated individuals to being understood as a *shared endeavor across campus constituents*. This is true with regard to not only shared planning and action, but also shared responsibility and accountability for making progress toward a set of coordinated, campus-wide goals. The latter involves moving from traditional notions of external evaluation to building capacity among campus constituents to conduct evaluation.

Practically, diversity work must move from isolated programs and course offerings to a network of policies and actions, including policies and actions around evaluation. In order to improve practice, meet goals, and ensure institutional viability, these efforts must be inextricably tied to institutional mission and purpose and should foster not only learning about the skills and content *of* diversity, but also awareness about what works and what does not work.

Comprehensive Diversity Work: Lessons from California

Scholars have noted that California serves as a "bellwether for other states" when it comes to diversity in higher education. California "has been a harbinger of policies for the United States, good and bad, that have had enormous social consequences" (Gándara, Horn, and Orfield 2005, 256), including the now infamous Proposition 209, which helped dismantle affirmative action in admissions on many campuses. The state's racial/ethnic diversity also makes it distinctive while again situating it as a harbinger for the nation. California has substantially higher percentages of Hispanic/Latino, Asian, and multiracial individuals than the nation as a whole.[2] This diversity also includes a sizeable immigrant population drawn primarily from Latin America and Asia.[3]

What are the specific lessons to be learned from California with regard to diversity in higher education, particularly for this new vision for diversity that places it at the center of institutional functioning? Answers to this question form the basis of this monograph, which developed out of the Campus Diversity Initiative (CDI), a project involving twenty-eight independent California colleges and universities organized and funded by the James Irvine Foundation between 2000 and 2005.[4] The CDI was designed to

---

[2] According to the U.S. Census Bureau, in 2004, 12.1 percent of California's population was Asian, compared to 4.2 percent nationally. Nearly 35 percent was Hispanic/Latino, compared to 14.1 percent nationally. California's multiracial population was 2.4 percent compared to 1.5 percent nationally. Of all the major racial/ethnic categories, only white and African American/black populations had lower percentages than the national average. See quickfacts.census.gov/qfd/states/06000.html.

[3] According to the 2000 Census, 26.2 percent of California's population was foreign born and of that population, more than 55 percent was born in Latin America and nearly 33 percent was born in Asia. See factfinder.census.gov.

[4] As part of the agreements for use of institutional data, none of the campuses are individually identified in the body of the monograph.

foster the conceptual and practical shift toward comprehensive diversity work that had, at its core, evaluation and organizational learning.[5]

Campus diversity has been a strong focus of the work of California's James Irvine Foundation for more than twenty years. In particular, the foundation has been committed to "working with colleges and universities to ensure that students, faculty and curricula at campuses reflect the state's diversity, and that all college students are prepared for participation and leadership in a diverse society."[6] After undertaking a review of its first ten years of grant making (Smith 1997), the foundation affirmed its emphasis on diversity in its higher education program and in 2000, developed the CDI.

Under the CDI, three-year grants were directed at creating institution-level change to (1) enhance college access and success for underrepresented minority (URM) and low-income students, and (2) build campus capacity to enhance and evaluate overall diversity efforts in ways that promoted organizational learning.[7] The foundation invited independent colleges and universities within the state to submit institutional overviews of the status of diversity efforts based on extensive self-studies that each campus completed. Once the foundation determined that a campus self-study indicated a readiness to engage in institution-level change in the two areas mentioned above, the campus was invited to submit a grant proposal. Over the course of the project, the foundation worked with campus leaders from twenty-eight institutions to develop grant proposals that clearly articulated institution-level goals for diversity, strategies for achieving goals, and a plan to evaluate progress.[8] Seven cohorts of campuses received grants between 2000 and 2003.[9]

The twenty-eight campuses in the CDI ranged from selective research universities to liberal arts colleges to small, special-mission institutions.[10] While these colleges and universities constituted less than one-third of all four-year independent, non-profit, accredited higher education institutions in California, they enrolled more than

---

5 Organizational learning takes into consideration the *process* of the work and requires *action* to ensure progress toward goals by making adjustments or corrections to the process as needed. Unlike evaluation models that are designed simply to catalog program activities, an organizational learning model shifts the focus to the effectiveness of the effort *to achieve desired outcomes* (Hernandez and Visher 2001; Preskill and Torres 1999).

6 See www.irvine.org/grants_program/former/higherEd/higherEd.shtml. In this monograph, the term "the foundation" is used when describing actions taken by the foundation's staff members and leaders. In addition, given that the CDI focused largely on institutional-level processes, the terms "the campus" and "campuses" are used when referring to processes that the ERT believed should be the shared responsibility of a broad cross-section of campus constituents.

7 In these pages, as within the CDI itself, the term "underrepresented minority" (URM) refers to African American, Latino/a, and American Indian/Alaska Native populations. When other minority groups are included, the term "people of color" or "students of color" is used.

8 A summary of CDI campus strategies can be found in appendix 1.

9 At the time of the writing of this monograph, the later cohorts were still completing their proposed work.

10 Twelve of the campuses had a religious affiliation, including eight Catholic institutions. Eight were doctorate degree–granting institutions, ten were master's degree–granting institutions, nine were baccalaureate liberal arts colleges, and one was a graduate/professional school. All but four campuses had received prior diversity grants from the foundation. Student population sizes ranged from less than 500 to 16,000 undergraduate students. Thirteen campuses had less than 1,200 students, ten had 1,200 to 3,500 students, and four had more than 3,500 students. One institution enrolled only graduate students.

60 percent of all undergraduates in such institutions.[11] The campuses varied greatly in size, selectivity, resources, and geographic location within California, and these variations influenced both the selection and implementation of strategies the campuses used to achieve institutional goals for diversity.

The CDI placed a particular emphasis on evaluation as a strategy for raising the level of institutional success with diversity work. The evaluation component had become increasingly important to the James Irvine Foundation for several reasons. The foundation had discovered that in prior funded initiatives, many campuses focused on implementing programs and projects and neglected to develop the means to evaluate institution-level progress. In addition, there were broad concerns in the philanthropic community about accountability and good stewardship. Many foundation leaders had begun to ask whether evaluation processes could be designed to facilitate organizational learning and help an institution make progress toward goals (Dowd 2005; Pew Charitable Trusts 2001; W. K. Kellogg Foundation 1998). As Campbell and McClintock (2002, 8) asked, could evaluation be used more to "improve . . . than to prove?"

The approach adopted by the foundation was to help the campuses build capacity to evaluate their diversity initiatives in ways that would allow them to learn from their experiences and make adjustments and mid-course corrections to improve their efforts. Once campuses developed the capacity to evaluate diversity initiatives, the foundation would have much of the information it needed to assess its grant-making strategy and the overall impact of its grants.

In 2000, the foundation contracted with Claremont Graduate University and the Association of American Colleges and Universities (AAC&U) to oversee evaluation efforts within the CDI. Called the CDI Evaluation Project, these efforts sought to (1) help the campuses build capacity to conduct meaningful evaluation of their diversity initiatives and (2) assess the overall impact of the CDI. These efforts were led by an evaluation resource team (ERT) composed of Claremont Graduate University and AAC&U staff, other experts in diversity and evaluation, and graduate research assistants. Senior members of the ERT served as liaisons to individual campuses.

This monograph is grounded in the diversity initiatives and the evaluation work conducted by the twenty-eight campuses as well as the analysis and expertise provided to them by the ERT. It reflects the lessons learned from the CDI and is designed to help guide institutions in planning, implementing, and evaluating comprehensive diversity work that has a focus on increasing access and success for URM and low-income students as well as building capacity to enhance and evaluate overall diversity efforts in ways that promote organizational learning.

Chapter 1 tells the story of the CDI and of the campuses as they went through their three-year grant projects. Campus leaders were required to monitor progress—setbacks as well as successes—to better meet their goals. They were also encouraged

---

11 Source: California Postsecondary Education Commission online data system, www.cpec.ca.gov/OnLineData/OnLineData.asp.

> **The Campus Diversity Initiative (CDI) at a Glance**
>
> Goals of the CDI—undertaken by teams from twenty-eight independent California institutions through three-year grants from the James Irvine Foundation
>
> 1. Enhance college access and success for URM and low-income students
> 2. Build campus capacity to enhance and evaluate overall diversity efforts in ways that promoted organizational learning
>
> Goals of the CDI Evaluation Project—undertaken by the ERT through a five-year contract with the foundation
>
> 1. Assist the twenty-eight campuses in building capacity to conduct meaningful evaluation of their diversity initiatives
> 2. Assess the overall impact of the CDI for the foundation
>
> Role of the campus liaison—undertaken by senior ERT members with expertise in diversity, evaluation, and organizational learning
>
> 1. Provide assigned campuses ongoing assistance in planning, implementing, and learning from their specific CDI evaluation
> 2. Collect and analyze data on campuses' progress to determine the overall impact of the CDI

to think about how access and success for underrepresented students fit into a much broader and more cohesive vision of diversity. This conceptual and practical shift took some adjusting, but by utilizing a comprehensive framework to implement diversity efforts, many of the campuses moved from "project-itis" toward greater coherence.[12] Given the time it took them to adjust to the new approach and the relatively short grant period, the campuses ended up making more progress in developing the *infrastructure* to generate success than in generating success itself, though many of the institutions began to make a demonstrable difference. Questions that remain as the CDI concludes are whether the campuses can maintain the new approach, continue their improvement efforts, sustain what they know works to foster underrepresented student success, and truly place diversity at the heart of institutional functioning.

Chapters 2 and 3 discuss the ERT's findings about the impact that the CDI had on campus diversity efforts. Chapter 2 summarizes six *quantitative* findings based on data submitted annually by the campuses through data workbooks. These findings reflect campus efforts that were largely focused on access and success of underrepresented students as well as work done by many of the campuses to increase the presence of URM faculty. Chapter 3 focuses on thirteen *qualitative* findings based

---

12 "Project-itis" refers to a proliferation of projects that do not necessarily tie in to larger institutional goals or other activities on campus. Project-itis may be occurring when constituents complain about "yet another initiative" springing up on campus, particularly if the initiative lacks clear goals, fails to build on existing diversity work, or goes forward without a plan for sustainability.

on data obtained by the ERT during campus site visits as well as data related to the degree of institutionalization of diversity work at the campuses.[13] This chapter specifically focuses on aspects of organizational learning shown to be important in enhancing overall institutional functioning related to diversity. Both chapters include campus examples that are intended to help other institutions meet with success in planning, implementing, and evaluating comprehensive diversity work.

Chapter 4 discusses promising practices that emerged from both the quantitative and qualitative findings and include recommendations about policies, programs, and planning for sustainability. The practices highlighted relate to the four dimensions of Smith's (1995) diversity framework and encompass a number of the concrete actions CDI campus constituents took to better ensure institution-wide success.

Chapter 5 offers a step-by-step guide to comprehensive diversity work for the broader higher education community. Though no single institution in the CDI reached high levels of success in all areas of the work, findings and promising practices taken from across all twenty-eight campuses—and from other campuses known to the ERT—cohere into a process that can give direction to other institutions' actions.

The conclusion draws the main text to a close by discussing the state of diversity at the present moment as colleges and universities continue to move forward in this new century. With recent action to roll back affirmative action policies in admissions and hiring, campus diversity work has come to a point where efforts could progress, stagnate, or regress. Elements described within this monograph—including an institution-wide framework for action and a process for evaluation and organizational learning—offer a way for campus diversity work to move forward with new vision and vitality to meet the needs of a changing population, society, and world. A set of resources at the end of this monograph will also help campuses undertake this comprehensive work.

This monograph illustrates how campuses can move away from diversity efforts that are piecemeal reactions (e.g., to external forces, such as anti-affirmative action legislation or even grant awards) and proceed toward proactive and comprehensive actions that foster both organizational and individual learning. The specific hope is that this monograph will help higher education leaders implement, evaluate, and continually learn from the experience of administering a comprehensive campus diversity initiative that is focused, in part, on increasing access and success of URM and low-income students. The larger hope is that it will guide leaders in helping all people attain a high-quality education that prepares them for participation in a diverse society and ensuring that colleges and universities continue to be viable contributors to that society.

---

13 "Institutionalization" here refers to the degree to which the work (1) reflected progress on achieving goals, (2) was sustained over time by the institution, and (3) evolved to meet new and sometimes unanticipated needs and challenges. The ERT developed a rubric to help examine the degree to which diversity had become institutionalized at the CDI campuses, in the areas of goals, resources, capacity, leadership, and centrality (see appendix 2).

Chapter 1
The Journey from "Project-itis" to Coordinated Action

The initial cohorts of colleges and universities participating in the James Irvine Foundation's Campus Diversity Initiative began their work in 2000. The process of helping each campus move toward comprehensive diversity work that fostered organizational learning unfolded in the first fifteen months of the project and was shaped by interactions with the different cohorts. During this time, these campuses and the ERT both learned a great deal about what worked and what didn't work in establishing an evaluation process that was manageable and that could be sustained post-grant.

By 2000, the foundation recognized that future diversity grants needed to place a much greater emphasis on evaluation, not just to judge the impact of the funding, but also to assist campuses leaders in using evaluation results—evidence of setbacks as well as successes—for learning and improvement. The foundation sought expert assistance in overseeing this evaluation component by inviting proposals from higher education researchers who had demonstrated experience with evaluation, diversity initiatives, and organizational learning. The foundation selected a collaborative approach offered by Claremont Graduate University and AAC&U. Their proposal included formative and summative approaches to helping campuses in their evaluation efforts and included as a key outcome the establishment of organizational learning as a campus norm.

The CDI Evaluation Project's work was undertaken by the ERT, a group comprised of Claremont Graduate University and AAC&U staff and other national experts in diversity and evaluation who were knowledgable about the philosophy and theory behind organizational learning.[1] The ERT's proposed work was distinguished by a commitment to help the campuses help themselves. As a resource team, the ERT would guide the campuses in developing their own capacity to conduct robust evaluation rather than serve as an external team that would evaluate campus projects "from the outside." As part of this arrangement, each campus was assigned a senior ERT staff person to serve as a liaison throughout the three-year grant period.

---

1   For more on this theory, see www.infed.org/biblio/organizational-learning.htm as well as Shafritz, Ott, and Jang 2005; Hernandez and Visher 2001; Preskill and Torres 1999; and Senge 2006.

First Steps

Leaders at four-year, independent California colleges and universities who were interested in obtaining grant funds under this reenvisioned strategy were invited to meetings between 2000 and 2003 where they received information about the new approach to diversity and evaluation. The majority of campuses that attended a meeting elected to participate in the new process, which involved three stages. Working closely with the foundation and the ERT to refine processes and documents at each stage, interested campuses would

- submit an **institutional self-study** that reflected on past diversity work and considered what next steps would accomplish the goals of the CDI in ways that were specific to the institutional context and that built on previous work;
- submit a **grant proposal** that detailed this next phase of diversity work and included a brief description of how campus leaders would track progress;
- submit **six-month reports** and **annual data reports** on progress made toward campus-specific goals, including a **detailed evaluation plan** that would accompany the first six-month report.[2]

A total of twenty-eight campuses were awarded grants by the CDI in seven cohorts staggered over three years. Participation required campus leaders to think and act in much more comprehensive ways about diversity work. For example, some campus proposals relied on a single person or small group of people to carry out the campus initiative. It was clear that such limited involvement would produce neither comprehensive outcomes nor the organizational learning necessary to make adjustments and mid-course corrections. In a letter from the foundation, campus leaders were urged to develop a broad-based team of people who would oversee the CDI, including evaluation efforts, and who would work directly with the ERT liaison. The campuses responded by creating teams that involved an array of constituents.

The early intervention and ongoing assistance had at least three benefits for the campuses. First, early intervention provided campuses with information and expertise in advance of specific program development, including research about what works (or had the potential to work) and why. Second, early guidance from the ERT helped campuses shape program components so that they could be *operationalized* and *measured over time*, thereby avoiding the difficulty of developing measures after the fact. Third, as program and evaluation strategies were implemented, the assistance provided during data collection and analysis gave campus leaders valuable information to enhance their efforts.

Some campuses were successful in establishing robust evaluation processes, but others were much less successful. Campuses with greater success benefited from a collaborative relationship that developed between the institution, the foundation, and the ERT. The collaboration reinforced the use of evaluation processes that would generate

---

2 Because of timing of grant cycles, the first cohort was funded before the ERT was assembled and the evaluation and reporting process was in place. As a result, this cohort did not work with the ERT through the three stages, as subsequent cohorts did.

three levels of organizational learning. At the institutional level, campus leaders would have information they needed to make adjustments and corrections to their strategies to achieve goals for diversity. At the foundation level, the ERT would have information it needed to assess the effectiveness of the foundation's overall grant-making approach. At a broader level, the ERT would have information that would help other colleges and universities avoid some of the pitfalls these institutions experienced and better translate promising practices to specific contexts.

In cases where there was limited success, campus leaders struggled to move away from perceiving underrepresented students as in need of "fixing" and from creating yet another program in order to do so. For example, in developing its institutional self-study, one campus team simply reported on all previous Irvine-funded projects and asked various departments to submit "wish lists" of next steps. Without having a broader vision, the departments generated lists of isolated retention programs for URM students. It took several iterations for this campus to move from the self-study phase and be invited to submit a proposal.

Shifting the Conceptual and Practical Work of Diversity on Campus

Over the five-year period of the CDI Evaluation Project, the ERT witnessed a shift in how campus leaders thought about and undertook diversity work. This shift related to both the number of people involved (from small groups of people to a growing commitment across campus) and the type of action that occurred (from isolated programs to a network of policies and actions). And a shift occurred in evaluation as well, as campus constituents learned how to gather, analyze, and share data that helped inform and improve practice.

Still, these shifts were not easy. Since 1987, most of the CDI campuses had done quite well in fulfilling the requirements of the foundation's diversity grants by merely reporting that they had done what their grant proposals said they would do. Now they were being asked to examine their past in order to chart their future, based on goals that could not be achieved by a single person or small group. This more broad-based level of work implicitly, if not explicitly, called for the campus to be more collaborative and coordinated. And with broader involvement also came broader accountability for outcomes.

The new approach required campus leaders to move from thinking about diversity as an end goal related to the composition of the student body to thinking about diversity as an opportunity for organizational learning that was connected to institutional mission. The most difficult part of this change involved how a campus would report on progress. Campus leaders needed mechanisms that would help them evaluate if and how progress in diversity work made a difference in achieving their institution's mission. These mechanisms included an institutional self-study, a proposal, and an evaluation plan, as well as six-month reports and annual data reports.

Institutional Self-Studies

Leaders from the twenty-four campuses that had received prior funding from the James Irvine Foundation were accustomed to reporting on institutional diversity efforts. Most often, these reports consisted of descriptions of promised deliverables—scholarships given, URM graduate fellows and faculty hired, and programs carried out. The design of these reports positioned the campuses to compete for future grants but did not compel them to learn about what worked and what did not work. In contrast, the CDI self-study was designed so that campus leaders could determine what needed to be done to increase the success of their efforts.

The most effective of the CDI self-studies were from campuses that broadly engaged campus constituents in developing the story of past work, determining steps to greater success, and detailing how the campus would know it was making progress. This required that constituents reflect on the experiences and the outcomes of their diversity work, which revealed both strengths and weaknesses. Some campuses struggled to create a coherent picture of their future diversity work because they could not envision doing diversity work comprehensively. Others struggled with creating a story of the past because prior efforts had consisted of isolated activities carried out by small numbers of people. In these cases, campus diversity work was particularly vulnerable to failure due to personnel transitions and loss of institutional memory.

A campus was invited to submit a grant proposal only after the self-study demonstrated that leaders had learned from their past work what future actions they needed to take to increase their levels of success. The self-study proved to be one of the most useful parts of the foundation's new approach because it challenged campus leaders to move toward a more intentional and coordinated approach to their diversity work or risk not being invited to participate in the CDI.

Grant Proposals

At the proposal writing stage, the first task was for campus leaders to articulate *specific* strategies that would make up the next steps in the institution's diversity work. This phase was made easier in cases where campus leaders had worked with a broad base of constituents on the self-study. In these cases, leaders could turn to constituents for assistance in developing strategies that built on the best elements of previous work and that filled gaps in existing efforts. Still, a few campuses had difficulty in laying out a set of actions that would address the capacity-building goal of the CDI because they had not yet connected the various pieces of their diversity work into a coherent whole.

Evaluation Plans

The evaluation plans were intended to help campus leaders focus attention on the appropriateness of their strategies and how they would measure progress toward institutional goals for diversity. Initially, campuses were asked to submit their plans with the self-studies, but the ERT found that campus leaders struggled with developing straightforward techniques to monitor progress. The ERT found it more fruitful for campus leaders to submit their plans with the first six-month reports, which provided more time for leaders to ensure that what they developed was manageable. In addition, the later deadline enabled campus leaders to focus simultaneously on their proposals, which established goals that reflected institutional mission and sound strategies to achieve the goals, and their plans, which would detail how they would ascertain that progress was being made.

Even though the timing change provided opportunities for greater focus, many campus leaders still found it difficult to develop manageable and sound evaluation plans. In some cases, campuses moved forward even though the plans were problematic. The ERT felt that continual revisions would not be as helpful as the experience of implementation.

Six-Month Reports and Annual Data Reports

Each campus created six-month reports that charted progress being made toward goals for diversity as well as lessons learned in the process. The reports were directed primarily at other campus constituents in order to raise awareness about the CDI across the institution. They were directed secondarily at the foundation and the ERT, to chart progress of the CDI across the twenty-eight institutions.

The early six-month reports revealed that creating user-friendly, reflective documents was a huge challenge for some leaders. Early reports were often dissertation length, full of anecdotal information about various projects, and focused solely on success stories. Such reports did not serve the campuses or the foundation well when the goal was to learn from their actions so that improvements could be made. The foundation and the ERT encouraged leaders to shorten their reports, gear them more toward campus constituents, and "tell all" so that the campuses could also learn from missteps that occurred.

Leaders needed time to become comfortable with revealing their missteps. In many contexts, "telling all" created anxiety that campuses might not receive future funding. Instead, the foundation hoped that leaders would examine their implementation processes closely and make necessary adjustments in order to improve access and success for underrepresented students as well as enhance overall diversity efforts. As importantly, the foundation hoped that organizational learning would become an enduring mode of operation beyond the grant period.

The six-month reports provided qualitative indications of progress, while the annual data reports provided quantitative information on progress. The data reports focused on a number of indicators, disaggregated by race/ethnicity and, where possible, income level. These indictors included first-year student enrollment and overall undergraduate student enrollment, faculty and administrative hires, and the composition of campus governing boards. The ERT requested that campuses also submit data that would indicate the relative level of success of URM students.

Most leaders struggled with providing concise, meaningful reports geared toward others on campus. Many struggled just to provide basic data because their campus did not have an institutional research office. Some early data reports consisted of dozens of pages of raw data, and some failed to disaggregate data. In response, the ERT curbed its effort to collect more sophisticated data across the CDI campuses to enable leaders to fully disaggregate at least some basic data.[3]

On the Road to Organizational Learning

The journey toward organizational learning involved helping campus leaders understand how to do comprehensive diversity work, collect and disaggregate data over time to chart progress, and use results to make adjustments to institutional processes and practices. The ERT provided technical assistance and resources to help facilitate organizational learning, including a comprehensive diversity framework, an assigned liaison to each campus, an annual evaluation seminar, guidance at national diversity conferences, and feedback on evaluation efforts throughout the grant period.

Diversity Framework

A search of the higher education literature yields numerous frameworks for charting and monitoring diversity efforts (e.g., Hurtado et al. 1999; Smith 1995; Williams, Berger, and McClendon 2005). The ERT used Smith's (1995) framework for diversity and its related institutional indicators to analyze the overall impact of the CDI across the twenty-eight campuses. The ERT also recommended that the individual campuses use this same framework to help them chart and monitor their efforts, and many did so.

The framework depicts four dimensions of diversity—institutional viability and vitality, access and success, campus climate and intergroup relations, and education and scholarship (see fig. 1). *Institutional viability and vitality* characterizes an institution's capacity to plan, implement, and evaluate comprehensive diversity work and encompasses the human, intellectual, physical, and fiscal resources needed to support such work. *Access and success* relates to an institution's undergraduate and graduate populations by field and levels, student success (e.g., graduation, performance, persistence, and honors), pursuit of advanced degrees, and transfer among fields, especially science, technology, engineering, and mathematics (STEM) fields. *Campus climate and intergroup relations* encompasses the type and quality of social interactions among students, faculty, and staff as well as individual and group perceptions of institutional commitment to diversity. *Education and scholarship* involves not only the availability of courses with significant diversity content, but also diversity course-taking patterns, faculty engagement with diversity issues, and student learning outcomes related to diversity.

The framework provided users with a way to broadly conceptualize diversity work on campus, and it also helped individuals on campus see how their work and their

---

3 In the concern over getting basic data disaggregated by race/ethnicity and income level, the ERT did not require that the data also be disaggregated by gender. Although collection of such cross-disaggregated data may have been unmanageable for some campuses, the information would have provided a richer picture of differences in outcomes between URM males and females—an area of inquiry in need of deeper examination (Harper 2006).

Figure 1. Framework for evaluating diversity

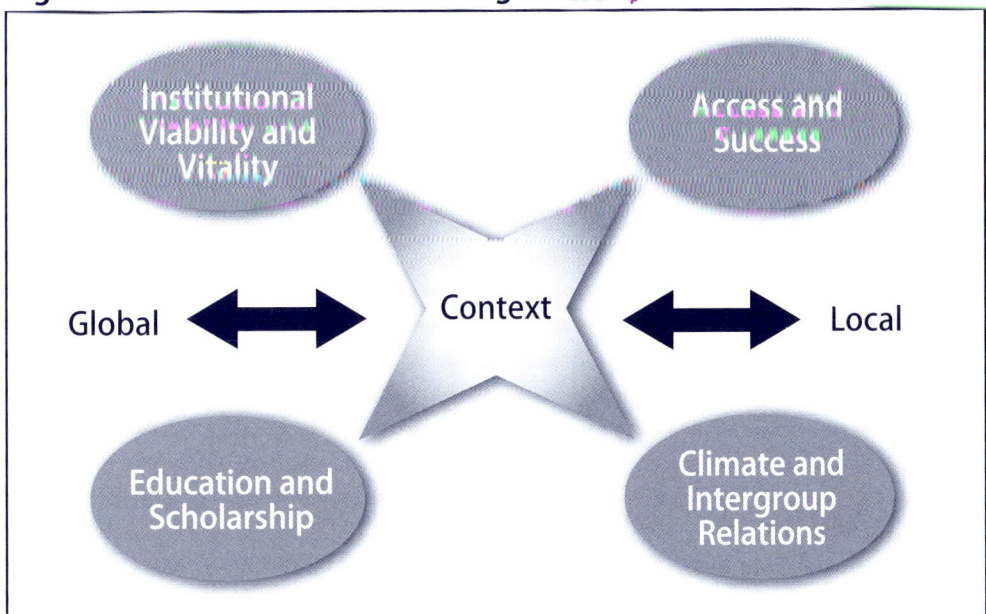

unit's work related to institution-level goals for diversity.[4] The institutional indicators, in particular, offered a means to measure progress on goals (see fig. 2).

While the focus of the CDI was on access and success of URM and low-income students (dimension one), the initiative located the responsibility for this work at all levels and across all units of the institution (dimensions two, three, and four). The foundation and the ERT realized that if campus leaders focused solely on student access and success, the strategies developed would likely be programmatic in nature and oriented toward "fixing" students rather than transforming the institution. It was clear that student success and institutional capacity were inextricably connected and that attention to each was critical.

The framework was also helpful in providing an orientation to diversity that was both inclusive and differentiated—it allowed campuses to focus on increasing access and success for URM and low-income students and also engage other aspects of diversity that were salient in their particular contexts. For example, the campus climate dimension invited investigations of student satisfaction and fit with respect to race/ethnicity and socioeconomic status, but also with regard to factors such as gender, religion, and sexual orientation. Likewise, under the education and scholarship dimension, CDI work could better weave issues of race/ethnicity and class into the curriculum, but a campus could also address matters of globalization and religion. An inclusive and differentiated framework could also illuminate other equity issues, such as differential levels of success among Asian American/Pacific Islander student populations.

---

4   The framework also reminded users that the compositional diversity of the student body was not the end goal unto itself, but rather part of a process of achieving larger goals for diversity.

Figure 2. Four dimensions of diversity—Institutional indicators

Institutional Viability and Vitality
- Institutional history of diversity issues and incidents
- Institutional strategies and dedicated resources
- Centrality of diversity in the mission and planning process
- Framework for monitoring diversity, with indicators
- Public and constituent perceptions of institution's commitment to diversity
- Board engagement with diversity and compositional diversity of board
- Compositional diversity of faculty and staff, by level

Education and Scholarship
- Availability (presence of diversity-related courses and requirements, degree to which courses include diversity issues, the placement of such courses)
- Experience (course-taking patterns of students)
- Faculty capacity (level of faculty expertise on diversity-related matters; number, level, and breadth of faculty participating in diversity efforts)
- Learning (quantity and substance of student learning about diversity)

Access and Success
- Undergraduate and graduate population by field and levels
- Student success (graduation, performance, persistence, honors)
- Transfer among fields (especially STEM)
- Pursuit of advanced degrees

Campus Climate and Intergroup Relations
- Type and quality of interaction among groups
- Perceptions of institution (commitment, engagement)
- Quality of experience and engagement on campus

Campus Liaisons

Each campus was assigned a senior member of the ERT who served as a consultant to the institution and functioned as a liaison between the institution and the larger ERT. The liaisons offered campus leaders ongoing guidance in developing and implementing their evaluation plans and collected qualitative data about campus progress. This qualitative information fed into the collective ERT efforts to help campuses move from a project orientation to an institution-level orientation. Liaison reports also constituted one important data source for the CDI impact study that ERT members produced for the foundation as well as for the larger audience of this monograph.

Annual Evaluation Seminar

The ERT organized annual evaluation seminars to provide information to the campuses on developing and implementing robust evaluation processes. The seminars also afforded ERT liaisons an opportunity to work directly with teams from their assigned institutions. In turn, the seminars gave campuses a chance to update the group on their diversity initiatives, address challenges, and share promising evaluation strategies.

Early campus cohorts offered advice to the group based on what they had learned from their experiences in establishing sound evaluation processes. The seminars also provided earlier and later cohorts with informal opportunities to discuss effective diversity practices.

National Diversity Conferences

The ERT realized early on that campus leaders needed to know much more about comprehensive approaches to diversity work and effective diversity programming. Since their primary focus was on helping the campuses build *evaluation* capacity, the ERT sought to build *knowledge* capacity by coordinating the participation of CDI campus representatives at national diversity conferences. At these conferences, campus representatives were encouraged to attend a wide variety of diversity-related sessions and directed to sessions related to evaluation. The ERT hosted special gatherings where representatives shared what they had learned in the conference sessions and reflected on a series of questions designed to help them connect what they learned to their campus efforts.

Feedback on Evaluation Processes

The campuses received several types of feedback about their work from the foundation and the ERT, including written reactions to their evaluation plans, written reactions to their six-month reports with recommendations for corrective action, and campus site visits by the ERT liaisons throughout the three-year grant period.[5]

Although the campuses and the ERT were able to document some progress in increasing college access and success for URM and low-income students under the new grant-making approach, there was more limited progress made in connecting diversity to all areas of institutional functioning and in adopting an organizational learning approach. However, this was not viewed as discouraging news for two reasons. First, three years is not much time for campuses to make such radical conceptual and practical shifts. This limited progress reflects only a snapshot of what eventually could be substantial, sustained progress. Only follow-up over time will tell. Second, a few campuses did make notable strides in establishing comprehensive diversity efforts within their three year grant periods, including establishing effective evaluation processes and using results for organizational learning.

On a positive note, the ERT uncovered a number of findings and promising practices and processes—outlined in the next four chapters—that will assist campuses in developing and evaluating comprehensive diversity efforts. As these next chapters attest, it is clear from the CDI that meaningful progress is likely to be achieved and sustained only if campuses locate diversity at the core of institutional functioning.

---

5 The ERT conducted site visits to half of the CDI campuses. All work with campuses concluded with the final evaluation seminar in November 2005, where the ERT presented preliminary findings of the impact study to campus representatives.

Chapter 2
Quantitative Findings

The Campus Diversity Initiative impact study (Smith et al. 2006), available online at www.irvine.org/assets/pdf/pubs/education/cdi_Eval_Impact_Study.pdf, includes extensive data tables and analyses primarily related to two dimensions of the diversity framework, access and success and institutional viability and vitality, and related indicators. This chapter provides a brief summary of those findings. To conduct these quantitative analyses, the ERT relied on data from campus data workbooks as well as data from the Integrated Postsecondary Education Data System (IPEDS) and other national and state sources. The indicators reported on were those for which disaggregated data could be collected from all or most of the twenty-eight campuses. In each case, data were averaged across a cohort of institutions to create a picture of overall progress.

URM and Low-Income Student Access

Within the access portion of the access and success dimension, the ERT analyzed data related to three indicators: (1) URM undergraduate student access, first-year and overall enrollment; (2) low-income undergraduate student access, overall and within racial/ethnic groups; and (3) URM graduate student access, where applicable. While American Indian/Alaska Native students are part of the URM population, special focus was given to this group with respect to the first indicator.

URM Undergraduate Students

Data obtained from the twenty-seven CDI campuses with undergraduate enrollments showed an increase in the racial/ethnic diversity of **first-year students** at most of the institutions between 2000 and 2004.[1] Growth in the number of URM students accounted for more than half (53 percent) of the 11 percent average growth in first-year students at these CDI campuses. Even though URM enrollment increased across the campuses by only 3 percent overall, URM students grew both in number and as a percentage of the total average population. Interestingly, the population of first-year "unknown" students grew by an average of 19 percent.[2]

There were noteworthy variations across the campuses and among different racial/ethnic groups over the period. Seventeen of twenty-seven campuses increased

---

1. As noted earlier, one campus had only graduate programs.
2. "Unknown" students are those that, for various reasons, fall into the category of "race/ethnicity unknown" in admissions/enrollment data. Findings from a related CDI research brief, *"Unknown" Students on College Campuses: An Exploratory Study* (Smith et al. 2005), suggest that a sizeable number of unknown students are white. See www.irvine.org/assets/pdf/pubs/education/UnknownStudentsCDI.pdf.

in overall number and percentage of URM students. Seven campuses increased in over all number of URM first-year students, but experienced a decline in percentage of these students as a result of an overall increase in class size. Twenty campuses increased in both number and percentage of Latino/a students, while eighteen campuses increased in both number and percentage of African American students. Thirteen campuses decreased in both number and percentage of American Indian/Alaska Native students, while five campuses increased in both number and percentage of these students.

Between 2000 and 2004, changes in **overall undergraduate enrollment** largely mirrored the patterns found in first-year enrollments. There was a consistent increase in the number of URM students in the overall undergraduate populations on most of the CDI campuses. The data show that the URM population increased, on average, from 20 percent to 22 percent across the twenty-seven campuses with undergraduate populations. This represented a 20 percent growth in the number of URM students. In addition, this 20 percent growth in URM students accounted for 36 percent of the total growth in undergraduates.

There was considerable variation across the campuses and among racial/ethnic groups with respect to overall undergraduate enrollments, making patterns difficult to discern. However, gains in Latino/a undergraduate enrollments were most consistent across the twenty-seven campuses, with nineteen campuses increasing in both number and percentage of these students.

American Indian/Alaska Native Students

Even within a focus on URM students, there is often a tendency to ignore American Indian/Alaska Native students because of the low numbers of these students on many campuses. Attention to these students is particularly important in California. Recent census data indicate that the total population of American Indians/Alaska Natives nationwide was 4.4 million, and of this number, just over 687,000 lived in California, the highest total of any state in the nation.[3] This represents 15.2 percent of the total American Indian/Alaska Native population (Lopez 2002).

The California population is a mix of many indigenous California tribal people and other North American tribal people, and data for California suggest that many American Indian/Alaska Native people are urban, rather than reservation-based, residents. Yet shockingly few attend California colleges and universities—they often constitute less than one percent of the student population at individual institutions. As mentioned, the CDI data indicate that five campuses had increased in both number and percentage of American Indian/Alaska Native students.

Low-Income Undergraduate Students

Economic barriers to higher education have been increasingly emphasized in discussions of access, but rarely have income status and race/ethnicity been examined

---

3 This includes individuals who listed more than one race. See www.census.gov/Press-Release/www/releases/archives/facts_for_features_special_editions/005684.html.

together. As part of the data collection for the CDI Evaluation Project, campuses were asked to provide data on Pell Grant recipients disaggregated by race/ethnicity.[4] Using available enrollment data from twenty-two of the CDI campuses, the ERT examined higher education access between 2000 and 2004 through two lenses—the distribution of Pell Grant recipients across racial/ethnic groups as well as the percentage of Pell Grant recipients within each racial/ethnic group.[5]

Analyses indicated that the number and average percentage of Pell Grant recipients declined overall, the latter from 26 percent to 23 percent. At the same time, URM Pell Grant recipients increased as an average percentage of all Pell Grant recipients, from 34 percent to 37 percent, while they decreased as an average percentage of all URM students, from 45 percent to 41 percent.

These findings, combined with data given above on URM student enrollments, suggest that much of the growth in URM student enrollments on these CDI campuses involved students who were not low income. While this did not mean that campuses were enrolling only high-income URM students, this is important information to know in order to monitor both the racial/ethnic diversity and economic diversity of the undergraduate student body.

URM Graduate Students

A subset of the CDI campuses offered graduate-level degrees, and as such, many of these campuses had diversity initiatives focused on increasing the access and success of URM graduate students. Data on graduate students were analyzed first for the eight doctorate degree–granting institutions in the CDI and then for the twelve predominantly master's degree–granting institutions.[6]

Between 2000 and 2004, the number of URM graduate students across doctorate degree–granting institutions increased slightly as an average percentage of total enrollment, from 12 percent to 14 percent. The largest growth was in Latino/a enrollment, which grew from 7 percent to 9 percent. In comparison, Asian American/Pacific Islander graduate students across these campuses decreased as an average percentage of total enrollments, from 12 percent to 11 percent. To put these numbers in context, IPEDS data show that in 1994, an average of 10 percent of graduate students at these institutions were from underrepresented minority groups and 9 percent were Asian American/Pacific Islander.

At the twelve master's degree–granting institutions, the average percentage of URM graduate students grew from 18 percent to 24 percent between 2000 and 2004,

---

4 The Federal Pell Grant program provides grants to low-income students within 150 percent of the poverty line. Although there have been concerns about the adequacy of Pell Grant status as an economic indicator, it is the best indicator to date for cross-institutional comparisons. Campus leaders should always examine their own data for a richer picture of the income status of their student body.

5 For more information on findings related to the intersection of race/ethnicity and income levels, see the related CDI research brief, *Using Multiple Lenses: An Examination of the Economic and Racial/Ethnic Diversity of College Students* (Moreno et al. 2006b) available at www.irvine.org/assets/pdf/pubs/education/insight_Multiple_Lenses.pdf.

6 This group includes the ten campuses classified as Master's degree–granting institutions plus two additional campuses that offered graduate-level programs.

while the average percentage of Asian American/Pacific Islander students grew from 5 percent to 9 percent during that same time period. Again, to put these numbers in context, IPEDS data show that in 1994, an average of 18 percent of graduate students at these institutions were from URM groups and 5 percent were Asian American/Pacific Islander, indicating no progress proportionally in the years just prior to the CDI. Interestingly, the growth in "unknown" graduate students at the doctorate degree–granting institutions (104 percent) contrasted sharply with the growth of this group at the master's degree–granting institutions (8 percent).

URM Student Success

As noted above, findings related to URM student success were largely based on data provided by the campuses. Ideally, campuses would have collected and analyzed disaggregated data on student majors, shifts between majors, and grade point averages, as these data would have provided a more complete picture of success. However, indicators of success were limited to fairly common measures—persistence and graduation data. The ERT obtained consistent data from most of the campuses on first- and third-year persistence patterns as well as four- and six-year graduation rates, disaggregated by race/ethnicity

Persistence

Many campuses focus on first semester and first- to second-year persistence, but the ERT believed that third-year persistence would be a better indicator of long-term student success. Overall, findings across twenty-three of the CDI campuses for which data were available indicated increased persistence among URM students and decreased gaps in third-year persistence among racial/ethnic groups between 2000 and 2004. Strikingly, for each entering cohort, Latino/a student persistence rates were the same as or better than the overall persistence rate at seventeen of the twenty-three campuses, while African American persistence was higher than overall persistence at nine of the campuses for the 2000 cohort and at thirteen of the campuses for the 2001 cohort. Yet the data also suggested that African American and American Indian/Alaska Native students were overall less likely to persist than other groups, particularly on campuses where student persistence was generally low. Finally, the data showed that the departure points varied among racial/ethnic groups. American Indian/Alaska Native students, Latino/a students, and white students tended to have a higher attrition rate after the first year. Trends on some campuses suggested that African American students were more likely to depart between the sophomore and junior years, and a few campuses experienced sizeable attrition of these students between the junior and senior year as well.

The ERT found that some of the CDI campuses did not focus on persistence beyond the first semester and first year, while a large number did not disaggregate their data by race/ethnicity. On these campuses, it was not possible for leaders to be intentional or strategic about their efforts to address persistence gaps. Yet these analyses also confirm that when campuses analyzed disaggregated data and focused their efforts on these crucial "departure points," they closed or greatly reduced gaps among groups.

Graduation

With regard to six-year graduation data, some findings from the 1997 student cohort (graduation by 2003) were noteworthy. Analyses across twenty-six campuses for which there were available data indicated that Latino/a students on many of the CDI campuses graduated at equal or higher rates than many other students. This was not the case generally for African American students, and graduation rates for American Indian/Alaska Native students fluctuated due to the small number of these students enrolled at these institutions. The reasons for these differing graduation rates warrant closer examination by individual campuses. Other data analyzed by the ERT suggested that these independent institutions had more students continuing through to the sixth year than popular conception might hold; it was not clear that the campuses were carefully examining this phenomenon and the impact it may have had on URM and low-income students.

Overall, gaps in persistence among racial/ethnic groups occurred at more selective as well as less selective institutions, suggesting that selectivity provided no guarantee of success in terms of persistence and graduation. Also, some less selective institutions with fewer resources reduced or eliminated gaps in graduation rates among racial/ethnic groups. This supports the argument that when data drives campus decision making about programs, strategies, and resources, student success is more likely to result.

Institutional Viability and Vitality

Of all the diversity efforts occurring nationally, increasing the racial/ethnic diversity of the faculty has been one of the least successful, yet it is critical in terms of the potential for effecting deep and lasting change. Increasing the number of URM faculty is critical if institutions are to remain legitimate and credible in their teaching and research functions. This urgency exists not only because of the faculty's role with advising and mentoring, but also because of evidence that a racially/ethnically diverse faculty contributes to (a) a broader research and teaching agenda, (b) greater variation in pedagogy, (c) building individual URM faculty members' credibility and leverage in institutional decision making, and (d) leadership that can influence institutions to meet the needs of a changing and increasingly diverse society (Center for Higher Education Policy Analysis 2004; Ibarra 2001; Maruyama and Moreno 2000; Milem 1999; Moreno et al. 2006a).

Within their work in this dimension, all of the CDI campuses focused some attention on increasing the racial/ethnic diversity of the faculty. The ERT's analyses focused on the period between 2000 and 2004 and on the hiring of tenured and tenure-track ("core") faculty at the twenty-seven CDI campuses for which the ERT had useable data.

Overall, URM faculty grew from 7 percent of the total faculty in 2000 to 9 percent in 2004—up from 5 percent in 1993. Hiring of Asian American/Pacific Islander faculty increased slightly overall, from 7 percent in 2000 to 8 percent in 2004. While the percentage of white faculty declined by 3 percent overall, the actual number of white faculty increased as a result of overall growth in the size of the faculty. The data mirror national patterns in tenured and tenure-track faculty in four-year institutions. Between 1993 and 2003, the percentage of URM faculty at four-year institutions grew only 2 percent nationally, from approximately 6 percent to 8 percent.[7]

Because a change in faculty composition was largely dependent on new faculty hires, the first analysis focused on hiring patterns of new faculty. Three questions were relevant: Were campuses hiring? Was the level of hiring high enough to make an impact? Was the racial/ethnic diversity of hiring at a sufficient level to have an impact on the overall racial/ethnic composition of the faculty?

CDI campuses were hiring at a substantial rate. On average, the total number of new core faculty hired between 2000 and 2004 at twenty-seven CDI campuses was 31 percent of the base number of total core faculty in 2000. The hiring rate on individual campuses ranged from 13 percent to 85 percent, with seven of the twenty-seven campuses hiring at more than 40 percent of the 2000 baseline. During this period, a total of 1,498 faculty were hired, averaging fifty-five faculty hires per campus. In addition, the size of the total core faculty increased 5 percent between 2000 and 2004.

Within this context of substantial hiring, URM faculty constituted an average of 12 percent of all new hires from 2000 to 2004. Asian American/Pacific Islander faculty also averaged 12 percent of new hires, and white faculty averaged approximately 68 percent of new hires. There was great variation among the campuses, with new URM faculty hires ranging from 0 percent to 29 percent of all new hires.

It became clear that the overall racial/ethnic composition of the faculty was not changing as fast as the rates of new hiring might have suggested. To understand this phenomenon, the ERT developed a formula to show the degree to which new URM hires were adding to the compositional diversity of the faculty or simply replacing URM faculty who had left. The faculty turnover quotient provided a simple means of highlighting the relationship between the racial/ethnic diversity of new hires and the overall change in faculty composition. It is provided in chapter 4 as a promising practice to monitor faculty racial/ethnic diversity.

The key finding here was that, on average, 58 percent of new URM faculty hires were going to replace departing URM faculty. In other words, nearly three out of five new URM hires simply replaced URM faculty who had left. In addition, approximately one-half of all new Asian American/Pacific Islander hires were going to replace departing Asian American/Pacific Islander faculty. Not surprisingly, campuses that made more progress in diversifying the faculty had lower turnover on average.

---

[7] "Faculty" here refer to tenured and tenure-track faculty only, for purposes of comparison with the schools in the current study. This 8 percent represents 25,250 URM faculty out of 319,280 tenured and tenure-track faculty. These data are from the IPEDS Peer Analysis System.

Chapter 3
Qualitative Findings

Over the course of the Campus Diversity Initiative, the ERT met regularly as a group and also organized annual evaluation seminars that included teams from the twenty-eight campuses. These meetings, along with regular electronic correspondence, allowed the ERT to also practice organizational learning—reflecting on the goals of the evaluation project, monitoring successes and setbacks in meeting those goals, and helping the campus make adjustments and corrections as needed. What emerged over the five years of close work with the campuses, reflection, and data analysis was a strong understanding of the "process" factors that influenced the levels of success campuses reached, both in implementing their strategies for comprehensive diversity work and in meeting the goals of the CDI.

The senior ERT members brought expertise in campus diversity work, evaluation, and organizational learning to the evaluation project. The thirteen factors described here span all four of the dimensions of Smith's (1995) diversity framework (see fig. 3) and reflect the senior ERT members' experiences working as liaisons to the CDI campuses as well as their prior work in diversity, evaluation, and educational change. Though the factors in all dimensions ultimately influence institutional viability and vitality, the five factors listed under viability and vitality clearly cut across all areas of campus functioning.

Understanding the Link between Diversity and Institutional History, Mission, and Culture

Many scholars have noted that an institution's past engagement with diversity affects the level of receptiveness for comprehensive work in the present (Hurtado et al. 1999; Milem, Chang, and Antonio 2005). Past experiences can be assessed in terms of the four dimensions of Smith's (1995) diversity framework to include, for example, a history of inclusion or exclusion of various groups of people, either by law or by tradition; past efforts to place diversity into the curriculum or have diversity-oriented scholarship valued in tenure processes; and a history of positive or negative relations in the classroom, residence halls, offices, and other environments where people interact. Awareness of these past experiences can help campus leaders understand where pockets of resistance or receptivity may currently exist as well as gauge overall institutional readiness for undertaking comprehensive diversity work.

Figure 3. Factors influencing the success of comprehensive diversity work, by dimension

Institutional Viability and Vitality
- Understanding the link between diversity and institutional history, mission, and culture
- Reducing fears and concerns that underlie resistance
- Developing leadership for diversity work throughout the institution
- Moving from "project-itis" to comprehensive, coordinated action
- Resolving the "quality versus diversity" debate

Education and Scholarship
- Recognizing and supporting pockets of success to build momentum and stimulate action
- Refocusing efforts from helping underrepresented students survive to ensuring that they thrive

Access and Success
- Raising awareness about inequitable practices
- Challenging myths associated with access and success
- Balancing attention to access with attention to success

Campus Climate and Intergroup Relations
- Gathering systematic accounts of URM and low-income student experiences
- Understanding the impetus behind diversity efforts
- Recognizing and compensating for burn out

Having a mission statement that reflects a commitment to diversity is essential. Many of the CDI campuses had missions that referenced diversity in some way (e.g., as part of a larger focus on social justice, as part of a commitment to graduating students who will be competitive in the work world, or as part of an interest in developing a diverse pool of leaders). Having diversity referenced in the mission announces to people on- and off-campus that diversity is part of the core academic enterprise and reaches across the whole institution in its focus. Its presence in the mission also sets the stage for assessment of diversity efforts, educational improvement efforts, and student success.

At the same time, just having this commitment reflected in the mission is not enough to mobilize constituents to engage in comprehensive diversity work. Although many CDI campus mission statements cited the importance of diversity, the ERT often discovered a disconnect between statements and actions. This was most evident on campuses that had little or no reference to diversity in their strategic plans, accreditation materials, program reviews, or capital campaign brochures—guiding documents for action at most institutions. Campuses must be willing to "live" all parts of the institution's mission and express their commitment to diversity through their planning efforts and everyday practices.

This task can be difficult because it involves examining, and often changing, the institutional culture. An organization's culture can be defined as the "values, assumptions, norms, and beliefs" (Williams, Berger, and McClendon 2005, 20) that exist within it and that are reflected in practices and processes. Diversity, in all of its iterations, can challenge the culture of an institution because it often sheds light on previously unexamined beliefs and practices.

Campuses would be wise to actively link diversity work to institutional history, mission, and culture from the beginning. Having an evaluation component that connects diversity efforts to educational effectiveness issues—for example, disaggregating student success data by race/ethnicity, income level, and gender—can also help place diversity work at the center of the academic enterprise.

Tackling change at all levels of organizational culture

Williams, Berger, and McClendon (2005) note that organizational culture comprises multiple levels. On a campus, the outermost levels consist of the most tangible elements (e.g., buildings, brochures, signs), which reflect "high levels of shared meaning" around their purpose and "are typically most easily modified" (20). The innermost levels (routine practices, espoused and embedded values and beliefs), in contrast, reflect "relatively little public, shared meaning" and are "the most intractable" (21). Elements that can be most easily modified, the authors note, often yield the most superficial kinds of change. The authors argue that in order to sustain deep and lasting change, such as the kind engendered by comprehensive diversity work, leaders must tackle *all levels* of organizational culture and pay careful attention to the levels of everyday practices, values, and beliefs. Leaders would also want to distinguish between core aspects of culture that need to change and those that do not. For example, they may decide to reframe notions of excellence, but maintain a commitment to rigorous achievement for all students.

Reducing Fears and Concerns that Underlie Resistance

Comprehensive diversity work that incorporates a strong evaluation approach faces many points of resistance. An institution-wide focus necessitates new ways of thinking and acting on the part of many individuals for whom isolated work is more familiar and accepted. Diversity, in particular, can evoke strong emotional responses from individuals about sometimes difficult topics and their own actions and behaviors. People can also experience general anxiety about change—even when the change in question is perceived as necessary or positive—especially when the change runs counter to someone's existing understanding of the world. Campus leaders may worry about "bad press" that might result from an evaluation approach that focuses on setbacks as well as successes. Individuals may be afraid that punitive action will follow if their work, or their unit's work, does not meet expectations.

With regard to diversity, campus leaders should be mindful of the powerful mental models and cognitive structures that people have for maintaining myths and stereotypes. People process novel information by drawing on their existing knowledge (Bransford, Brown, and Cocking 1999; Donovan, Bransford, and Pellegrino 1999). When that knowledge is built on a foundation of misinformation, myths, and stereotypes, the new information will often be filtered in ways that support existing understandings, even in the face of contradictory evidence. Only when *enough* counter-evidence exists will the new information or experience help diminish myths, stereotypes and misinformation, rather than reinforce them.

In working with the CDI campuses and in other settings, the ERT encountered all of these types of fear. Four types stood out as particular factors that influenced the success of comprehensive diversity work on the CDI campuses: fear that leads to stealth resistance, concerns about legal challenges, suspicion regarding evaluation and assessment, and anxiety about public scrutiny.

Fear that Leads to Stealth Resistance

Stealth resistors, in this context, are those who keep their views to themselves while acting in ways that challenge, undermine, or impede comprehensive diversity work. Because of this behavior, these resistors avoid the kind of public examination of their position that both overt resistors and advocates experience. This makes it difficult for campus leaders to effectively neutralize stealth resistors' influence on campus climate and decision-making processes. However, the ERT pointed out several remedies to the CDI campuses to help lessen the effects of this type of resistance.

- Leaders would be wise not to assume they have achieved *consensus* on important decisions that were passed by a *majority*. Sufficient time should be allotted during decision-making meetings for constituents to verbalize or write down their views—favorable or unfavorable—on action items as well as on the decisions that are ultimately made. Having views on record means that campus leaders can challenge subsequent actions if the actions are inconsistent with stated positions. In the case of unfavorable views, leaders can opt to review the decisions that are made, discuss the intent and goals of the action, and "name" the resistance in order to work through it.
- Leaders should not dismiss stealth resistors once they are discovered. When leaders dismiss them, resistors' discontent can sabotage efforts to build comprehensive diversity efforts.
- Leaders should instead engage resistors in constructive dialogues about their views. These dialogues often reveal misunderstandings and misinformation on the part of resistors as well as potential points of agreement, which in turn provide opportunities to build alliances.
- At the same time, it is wise for leaders to limit the amount of energy they expend persuading stealth resistors to engage in diversity work. Devoting a significant amount of time and attention to this group tends to wear out advocates. Indeed, on several CDI campuses, a number of advocates "burned out" before strong foundations could be laid for comprehensive diversity work.

Concerns about Legal Challenges

Legal challenges to diversity may very well be the largest single factor influencing the success of comprehensive work on campus, particularly aspects related to student access and success. The Supreme Court upheld the University of Michigan's admissions policies in *Grutter v. Bollinger* based on compelling, research-based arguments that demonstrated the educational benefits of a diverse student body (Cross 2002; Gurin 1999; Gurin, Lehman, and Lewis 2004). At the same time, the Court held that participation in programs could not be based *solely* on race. Campus leaders must resist using legal challenges (or the possibility of legal challenges) as an excuse to do nothing, or to take a wait-and-see attitude. Rather, campus leaders need to better understand the connections between comprehensive diversity work and their mission of educational excellence and make these connections transparent to campus constituents and the general public.

In the wake of these court cases, the ERT observed a national trend of campuses moving into "compliance mode" on work to diversify student and faculty populations. So pervasive was this movement that after the verdicts, one University of Michigan administrator noted, "One might have thought that we lost both our cases before the Supreme Court." Many campuses and philanthropies have either eliminated programs and scholarships designed to redress historical racial and ethnic inequities, or opened them to include people of all races under the threat of lawsuits from anti-affirmative action groups (Schmidt 2006). Given the minimal progress CDI campuses made in URM faculty hiring—and similar national trends—the ERT raised concerns about future efforts to meet institutional goals for diversifying the faculty. While it is still too early to ascertain the full impact of the Court's decisions in the Michigan cases, the continued press of anti-affirmative action groups will likely push campus leaders to reconsider significant aspects of their recruitment and retention plans if they do not obtain good guidance about how to legally sustain them (see Kim 2006).[1]

The CDI campuses were not immune to concerns about legal challenges, but some did employ strategies that are likely to help stave off such challenges. At one campus, leaders met frequently to review the language of the Court's decisions in order to chart positive directions for their institutional efforts within the accepted parameters of the rulings. Crucially, these leaders closely examined how their CDI efforts linked to institutional mission and also reviewed how constituents enacted initiative goals through curricular and cocurricular activities. For example, linking intergroup dialogues to coursework made the understanding of racial/ethnic differences an explicit part of campus learning objectives. This in turn lent credence to efforts to ensure a racially/ethnically diverse student body.

The ERT found that when CDI campus leaders inextricably linked their initiatives to student learning outcomes, to the role of higher education in creating a diverse pool of leaders, and to higher education's role in addressing complex social challenges, the campuses were better able to make the case for why it was important to use race/ethnicity as

---

1 A 2006 Michigan referendum banning affirmative action at the state's public colleges and in government contracting will likely become a model for anti-affirmative action groups in other states and impede campus diversity efforts. Indicating her resolve, University of Michigan president Mary Sue Coleman stated, "I am determined to do whatever it takes to sustain our excellence by recruiting and retaining a diverse community of students, faculty and staff" (Jaschik 2006).

one of several factors in undergraduate and graduate admissions, scholarship awards, programming efforts, and faculty recruitment and retention.

As institutions continue to build comprehensive diversity efforts in the wake of new Supreme Court appointments, it will be even more critical that campus leaders are able to provide sound evidence of the positive contribution diversity makes to all students' learning and preparation for work and life in an increasingly pluralistic society.[2] This means that leaders will need to establish outcomes and measurable indicators for diversity learning and competence.[3] Furthermore, they will need to articulate and demonstrate *how* outcomes are achieved—under what specific conditions and through what specific curricular and cocurricular activities. An organizational learning approach to monitoring progress of diversity efforts provides one of the best mechanisms through which to build this crucial evidence and to improve and sustain the work.

Suspicion Regarding Evaluation and Assessment

Suspicion is likely to be present on campuses where evaluation and assessment have been done poorly, where assessment results have been used to penalize individuals and units rather than to spark professional development and educational improvement, or where results have been ignored when funds for improvement were being allocated. In addition, recent focus on student success by state legislatures and groups such as the Commission on the Future of Higher Education has created general tension around testing and measurement.[4]

Some suspicion is also likely due to older evaluation and assessment models, which suggested that the only valid undertakings were those conducted by third parties (Ewell 2004). More recent work in this area suggests that rigorous program-embedded assessment models and institution-level evaluations are actually more valuable in terms of generating results that can be used for educational improvement and organizational learning (Shulman 2005; Williams and Wade-Golden 2006).

Campus leaders would be wise to acknowledge if and how previous evaluation and assessment efforts have been politicized and recognize that these processes can arouse fear if their purpose is to single out or punish a small group or individuals. Leaders must clearly articulate *why* these efforts are necessary to advance institutional goals, including the need to demonstrate the benefits of diversity—for individuals and for society—to the general public.

---

2 Through extensive conversation that AAC&U staff have had with the higher education and business communities, intercultural knowledge and competence has emerged as an "essential learning outcome" and part of the learning that all students need to be prepared for the challenges of a twenty-first-century global economy (AAC&U 2007; Ferguson 2005; Guinier and Torres 2002; Miller and Leskes 2005).

3 Competence includes the ability to interact across differences in principled and productive ways in the context of an increasingly diverse domestic and global workforce. Campus leaders would be wise to consult theory and research on intercultural competence as they establish the parameters for this outcome at their institutions. For more information, see Orfield and Whitla 2001 and Cross 2002.

4 For more information on the commission, see www.ed.gov/about/bdscomm/list/hiedfuture/index.html.

Anxiety about Public Scrutiny

Many campus leaders grow anxious at the mere mention of evaluation because it signifies a public airing of setbacks and failures that have occurred within their sphere of influence. For that reason, it is important to establish an evaluation process that is motivated by two principles: gaining greater understanding of the challenges faced and how they might be addressed, and including those affected by the evaluation in the work as much as possible. This will help to quell fears that the results will be used to simply punish those doing the work.

This does not mean that people should not be held accountable for achieving agreed-upon outcomes, but rather that accountability should "work both ways." In addition to holding responsible parties accountable for outcomes, campus leaders have a responsibility to inform various stakeholders of institutional expectations, provide ongoing resources and support to ensure that expectations are able to be met, and offer ongoing feedback about progress.

Developing Leadership for Diversity Work throughout the Institution

The experience of the CDI campuses reinforces the notion that leadership for comprehensive diversity work must include constituents from across campus and from all levels of the institution. The president, chief academic and student affairs officers, deans, faculty, staff, governing boards and students all have roles to play in these efforts. Likewise, leaders at different levels must be present to hold the people within their sphere of influence accountable for outcomes and ensure that those efforts align with, and connect to, institution-level goals. Finally, in order to ensure that decision making for the work is informed by direct experience, these leaders must also be actively involved in efforts in ways that are appropriate to their roles on campus.

Early in the project, there was a tendency for some of the CDI campuses to institute a single-person leadership model for campus-wide diversity work. This advanced the work when the person played a coordinating role, but *not* when the single leader was expected to do all of the work from one office. However, in most of these early instances, one person—often in student affairs—was solely *responsible for* and *accountable for* achieving the broad, multilayered goals that campuses had for their diversity initiatives. This was a recipe for failure. In these cases, the designated individual faced a task that exceeded what one person was capable of accomplishing, and he or she often lacked adequate time, resources, and/or credibility to deeply engage all constituents, particularly faculty, in the work. A model of effective leadership is discussed in chapter 4 as part of the promising practices.

> ### A Special Note about Large Institutions
>
> Large institutions with decentralized structures may be tempted to turn over the evaluation process to an institutional research office or similar unit. On the one hand, it is beneficial to draw on campus-based expertise and align the evaluation of comprehensive diversity work with existing evaluation processes. On the other hand, evaluation work is often more successful when a broad-based group of constituents is engaged in doing the work. If the monitoring effort is perceived as the purview of a single unit, the process may devolve into a report-production process rather than one that generates significant learning on the part of many people. To bypass this problem, when an institutional research office or similar entity is charged with the task of monitoring progress, staff would be wise to engage the broader community throughout the process—from the initial formulation of questions to be answered to the interpretation of evaluation results.

> ### Building an Inclusive Process to Monitor Comprehensive Diversity Work
>
> The processes campuses use to monitor their comprehensive diversity work are critical to the success of the effort, and the results may attract a great deal of attention from constituents. When campus leaders establish a broadly inclusive monitoring process, a greater number of constituents are likely to shoulder responsibility for achieving the overall outcomes of the work, and fewer would have cause to simply "point fingers" over negative results.
>
> The cross-section of constituents should be diverse, not only in terms of position and location on campus, but also in terms of race/ethnicity, gender, and other aspects of social identity. Campuses that lack appreciable racial/ethnic diversity within staff, faculty, and senior administrative ranks should be especially mindful to tap URM campus leaders for this work, though not to the extent that it overburdens a few individuals. Leaders should provide appropriate release time and rewards to individuals doing this work, and perhaps invite URM individuals from the community to participate. It is also critical that leaders involve those directly affected by evaluation results, including URM and low-income students.
>
> This cross-section of constituents should take part in the process of identifying (1) the desired outcomes, (2) indicators to measure achievement of the outcomes, (3) strategies to obtain data, and (4) ways to interpret and make meaning of the data. Deciding when and how the results will be shared more broadly should also be an open and inclusive process.

Moving from "Project-itis" to Comprehensive, Coordinated Action

When faced with the challenge of implementing and evaluating comprehensive diversity work, many campus leaders first look to divide the work to be done into projects that address different pieces of the challenge. This can lead to tremendous excitement on the part of constituents doing the work and result in innovative practices. However, all too often constituents focus so much attention on creating individual projects that the projects themselves—launching them and keeping them going— become the end goal. This has the effect of eclipsing the original, broader goals of the work. It also turns attention away from the time and effort needed to develop connections among the individual projects and between the projects and larger institutional goals for diversity.

ERT members observed this tendency many times on CDI campuses and elsewhere. For example, one ERT member visited a college that instituted a diversity theater project to increase campus dialogue about issues related to race and ethnicity. The project directors reported that the performances were well attended and provoked productive discussion among participants. Yet, this ERT member noted that the project was not connected to larger institutional discussions about race/ethnicity or to broader institutional goals for developing students' intercultural competence. The result was an isolated program with little information related to its effect on student learning.

> ### Developing a Cure for Project-itis
>
> To help the campuses move from simply delineating programs and projects to focusing on broader goals for diversity, the James Irvine Foundation offered the following written feedback to CDI campuses early in the process: "We recognize that the Irvine-funded activities are only a piece of an overall picture. The [evaluation] plan should show how the pieces are connected. One approach that seems to work well is to (1) describe the overall institutional goals and outcomes, (2) indicate the role of the Irvine projects and other activities in achieving the goals/outcomes, and (3) identify how progress toward those goals/outcomes will be assessed. Please be sure you are assessing progress toward the ultimate goals/outcomes, not simply assessing whether the projects and activities took place."

Resolving the "Quality versus Diversity" Debate

Many times, campus leaders launch educational quality initiatives and diversity initiatives on parallel tracks without considering how these efforts inform and enhance each other. This is compounded by a persistent mindset among some campus constituents that diversity efforts lower educational quality, despite evidence to the contrary (Milem, Chang, and Antonio 2005; Williams, Berger, and McClendon 2005). Such notions can stem from a reliance on indicators of quality such as standardized test scores, which do not necessarily identify the talent necessary for academic success and leadership in society. They can also be fueled by insidious stereotypes about URM students related to intellectual inferiority and lack of motivation to study and learn.

Indeed, ERT members heard comments from administrators and faculty on the CDI campuses that greater compositional diversity would result in lowered educational quality. Campuses that addressed these issues openly found them difficult discussions to have, but they helped individual constituents move beyond stereotypes and helped the campus as a whole think about what counted as evidence of quality and continue to make progress on comprehensive diversity work.

Recognizing and Supporting Pockets of Success to Build Momentum and Stimulate Action

It is unrealistic to think that many campuses can—or should—"scrap" existing projects and start anew from an institution-wide action plan that is focused on broad goals and driven by evaluation. However, by clarifying goals, building an evaluation process, and identifying pockets of success, campuses can achieve the institutional coordination and coherence needed for their diversity work to truly be comprehensive. (For recommendations about how campuses can better integrate projects and other pockets of innovation, see Bauman et al. 2005; Milem, Chang, and Antonio 2005; and Williams, Berger, and McClendon 2005.)

Within the CDI, the self-studies helped the campuses avoid "recreating the wheel" wherever possible. In many cases, the self-studies directed campus leaders to strengthen coordinating structures between existing projects or enhance related evaluation efforts rather than develop new projects.

One "pocket" that gained momentum involved engaging faculty in diversity work through re-granting programs. By giving faculty the opportunity to apply for small grants to undertake scholarship, travel, curriculum revision, or campus-based seminars related to diversity, the programs enabled faculty to pursue academic and scholarly aspects of diversity in relation to their own interests. Many of the campuses redirected CDI funds to expand these programs once leaders realized that more faculty members wanted to participate than were able under the original funding allocations.

Learning a Lesson the Hard Way: Backing the Experts behind the Successes

On one CDI campus, leaders devised a re-granting strategy for faculty members who sought to infuse diversity into their curricular offerings. Ethnic studies faculty were excluded from this opportunity because leaders assumed that these faculty members had already accomplished this work. The ethnic studies faculty, on the other hand, wanted to refine what they had already accomplished and add new perspectives into their courses. These faculty members felt punished, in effect, for successes they had achieved at an earlier time, when diversity work was much less supported across campus. To add to their consternation, these faculty members were not incorporated into the re-granting process in any way. Several of them noted how their expertise would have helped in developing the criteria for the re-granting program and in the proposal review process. Campus leaders should recognize the expertise of individuals "behind" diversity work successes by supporting their continued progress and utilizing these individuals in planning, implementing, and evaluating institution-wide efforts.

Refocusing Efforts from Helping Underrepresented Students Survive to Ensuring that They Thrive

Over the past twenty years, many models and practices designed to support URM and low-income students have focused on retention. Unfortunately, these models and practices often resulted in persistence being the end goal for underrepresented students, rather than a necessary condition for them to participate in high-impact educational experiences, to achieve at high levels, and to develop as leaders.[5] The emerging emphasis on student learning outcomes provides an opportunity to address the historical tendency to make retention the primary measure of "success" for underrepresented students (for more information on the emerging consensus about essential learning outcomes, see AAC&U 2007).

In addition, many "remediation" models have focused on URM and low-income student deficits to the neglect of the assets these students bring to the educational enterprise.[6] Such deficit-oriented approaches may stem from stereotypes that exist in the larger culture and can also reinforce them. Furthermore, some scholars have argued that when these approaches rely solely on traditional input measures (e.g., SAT/ACT scores) to measure "deficit level," they do less to serve these students and more to "reproduce . . . dominant patterns of social stratification" (Williams, Berger, and McClendon 2005, 9).

Over the course of the CDI, the ERT discovered that programs focusing solely on retention and persistence often began with low expectations of URM and low-income students and seldom introduced students to aspects of the college experience that reflect high achievement, such as undergraduate research, departmental honors, or planning for graduate and professional school. Indeed, nationally, retention and persistence models rarely examine what is necessary for students to succeed at levels suitable for pursuing these opportunities, and ultimately, for assuming leadership in society and in the workplace (AAC&U 2007; Gándara, Horn, and Orfield 2005). On the other hand, program designs that set high expectations, empower students to successfully navigate the college environment, deeply engage them in their studies, and focus on learning and high achievement have the potential to not only boost URM and low-income students' self-efficacy but also shift how these students are viewed by the larger academic community (AAC&U 2002; Kuh et al. 2005).

Raising Awareness about Inequitable Practices

Examining the privileges embedded in existing institutional structures and how they shape campus policies and practices is an important task for institutions undertaking comprehensive diversity work. This is particularly true in areas related to access and success.

---

5 High-impact practices consist of curricular approaches such as learning communities, undergraduate research, and supplemental instruction that studies have shown to have positive effects on student learning and achievement. See Cross 2002 for more detail.

6 These assets include cognitive and non-cognitive capability, cultural background, life experience, understanding of systems of inequality, and perseverance in spite of adversity caused by these systems (Sedlacek 2004).

With regard to access, for example, many selective institutions produce student admissions ratings that reward the number of Advanced Placement (AP) courses taken. While admissions counselors may give a lower rating to students who do not take AP courses in schools where they are offered, counselors do not always account for the fact that some students attend schools without AP offerings. These schools tend to be in low-income districts that lack resources, and their graduates can be disadvantaged in comparison to students from more affluent high schools that offer many AP courses.

With regard to success, leadership scholarships often rely on traditional, "positional" notions of leadership in determining awardees.[7] This practice benefits students who have access to these opportunities and the resources to attain them.[8] Campus leaders may be unintentionally or intentionally shutting out students with other types of involvements, including significant job responsibilities, family responsibilities, or community responsibilities.

Additionally, when campus leaders lack data disaggregated by race/ethnicity and other relevant factors, they cannot ask themselves if all groups are succeeding. This can be particularly problematic when trying to address an absence of URM students in the STEM fields, in honors programs, and in programs related to planning for graduate and professional school. Ultimately, this lack of disaggregated data has a profound influence on the "pipeline" of future URM faculty as well.

Challenging Myths Associated with Access and Success

In working with constituents on the CDI campuses and elsewhere, ERT members encountered numerous myths related to access and success. Five of the most common myths are discussed below.

Myth #1:
The Student Body Is Racially/Ethnically Diverse—Mission Accomplished

When some of the CDI institutions reached a certain level of racial/ethnic diversity in the student body, many campus leaders felt that their mission had been accomplished. This focus on composition has been widely critiqued for being the end rather than the beginning of an institution's engagement with diversity (Milem, Chang, and Antonio 2005). Unfortunately, even campus leaders who consider compositional diversity to be part of broader diversity work often believe that the mere presence of a racially/ethnically diverse student body is sufficient to derive educational benefits. There are several problems with this line of thinking as well. It assumes that students (and others) are capable of interacting *productively* across differences, or have the wherewithal to develop this capability on their own. It assumes that they will interact regularly with people of different racial/ethnic backgrounds over time and that these interactions will result in a deeper understanding of themselves

---

7 This typically involves campus-based positions such as student government officer or residence hall council member and would not necessarily include students' leadership in their home communities, for example.

8 Access includes knowledge about the opportunities, and resources include not only monetary resources, but also time to devote to campaigns to attain leadership positions and develop applications for the awards.

and others. This leaves a great deal of the development of intercultural competence—a key outcome of a high-quality undergraduate education—up to chance.

Students are shortchanged in their preparation for work and leadership in a diverse society when institutions simply increase the enrollment of URM students. Campus leaders need to establish curricular and cocurricular activities that intentionally draw on the racial/ethnic backgrounds of all students to derive educational benefits for everyone—benefits such as increased cognitive complexity, reduction of stereotypes, multi-perspective thinking, and the ability to work in and lead diverse groups (see Milem, Chang, and Antonio 2005 for a fuller discussion of these educational benefits).

> ## Intentional Engagement of Differences: Intergroup Dialogues
>
> One common strategy to engage differences in the service of learning is an intergroup dialogue program. These programs facilitate dialogue among a set of students across some difference that carries social significance, such as race/ethnicity, gender, sexual orientation, religion, or class. Without this type of engagement, students may view these differences in simplistic or stereotypical ways. With appropriately guided discussion, students can come to understand the nuances to be found within these differences, how these differences have played out historically and for students in the room, and how social systems and institutions can have a differential impact on individuals and groups.
>
> Of course, the mere presence of an intergroup dialogue program does not guarantee these results. Dialogue groups should have highly skilled facilitators who can productively manage conflict, help students work through misunderstandings and reduce stereotypes, and challenge and support all students. From an institutional perspective, the program should carry significance by bearing credit for students, being woven into broader goals for the curriculum and for diversity, and involving faculty, staff, and students from across campus.

Myth #2:
Recruiting International Students of Color "Takes Care of" Compositional Diversity

At some of the CDI institutions, campus leaders sought to increase the racial/ethnic diversity of the student body by expanding the recruitment of international students of color. This was troubling for several reasons. First, this strategy ignored pressing issues concerning college access and success for U.S.-born students of color, particularly URM students. Second, it sent the message that all people of color are the same, or interchangeable. Third, the process often hinged upon international students' ability to afford private school tuition, bypassing issues of access for low-income students of color.

This does not mean that strategies to recruit international students of color are undesirable for institutions, but these should be distinct from strategies to recruit U.S.-born students of color. As myth #3 indicates, data need to be disaggregated not only by race/ethnicity, but also *within* racial/ethnic groups, to get a more complete answer to the question, "Who are our students?" Campuses can then take advantage of the presence of students of color from the United States and abroad to deepen all students' learning about differences within and among groups.

Myth #3:
We Can Diversify by Income and "Take Care of" Racial/Ethnic Diversity
Nationally, discussion about the lack of college access for low-income students has increased both in frequency and urgency. While this is an important step in terms of broadening college access generally, it also presents a powerful challenge. Many national experts, campus leaders, and politicians have begun to talk about class and income level in lieu of race/ethnicity, arguing or assuming that increasing access for low-income students will "take care of" access for URM students at the same time.

This is another problematic line of reasoning. It can reinforce a persistent stereotype that all underrepresented minority groups are from low-income backgrounds. It also reinforces the notion that campuses are unable to look at both factors—income level and race/ethnicity—at the same time.[9] The danger of dichotomous thinking is that institutions may ultimately turn attention away from the persistent disparities in access and success across racial/ethnic groups, especially in light of recent Supreme Court decisions regarding race as a consideration in admissions. Yet these disparities exist independent of disparities related to income level.[10]

The Importance of Analyzing Race/Ethnicity and Income Level Together

Recent analyses of data from the CDI campuses (Moreno et al. 2006b) suggests that institutions lose out on important information about their students when they view race/ethnicity and income levels in isolation from one another. Campus leaders run the risk of not understanding the extent of economic diversity within different racial/ethnic groups *or* the extent of racial/ethnic diversity within groups from different income levels. This lack of understanding has consequences for campus programs and support structures designed to assist underrepresented students. For example, some of the CDI campuses had sizeable gains in the number of URM students from middle-income and upper-income backgrounds, but many campus leaders were not aware of this because they did not examine data on income level and race/ethnicity together. As a result, these URM students were often steered toward services that focused on improving academic skills, a common need for many low-income students, when a bigger concern for many of them involved navigating a predominantly white campus.

---

9 For decades, scholars have argued that social class in America must be examined in the context of the particular histories of exclusion faced by people of color in the United States. Scholars too have noted the importance of looking at class as it *intersects* with race/ethnicity and other social identity dimensions such as gender and sexual orientation (Hill-Collins 2000; Crenshaw et al. 1996). This would allow campus leaders to consider, for example, how whiteness might shape the experience of being low-income for some students (Borrego 2003) and how racism and classism may combine forces to push some students toward dropping out more quickly.

10 For example, scholars have studied the influence of campus climate (e.g., Hurtado et al. 1999), stereotype threat (e.g., Steele 2003) and teacher expectations (e.g., Gay 2000; Gay 1994) on URM student success.

Myth #4:
Asian American/Pacific Islander Students Have No Barriers to Access or Success

The "model minority" myth was first used in the 1960s to explain the success of Chinese and Japanese groups (Lee 1996; Takaki 1989). This stereotype has since expanded to the point where individuals often assume that all Asian and Asian American/Pacific Islander students excel in their studies and in college generally. This myth masks the realities of more recent immigrants from Asian and Pacific Islander backgrounds, particularly since 1975. Asian and Asian American/Pacific Islander students regularly confront stereotypes, language barriers, cultural conflicts, racism, heavy work demands, and significant family responsibilities while navigating college. These experiences contrast considerably with the "model minority" myth.

Campus leaders may point to statistics on Asian American/Pacific Islander students that indicate comparable academic success to white students, but these statistics can mask considerable differences in access and success that exist *among* Asian and Asian American/Pacific Islander ethnic groups. For example, researchers have begun to gather specific data on Southeast Asian American students. These students—Cambodian, Chinese-Vietnamese, Hmong, Lao, and Vietnamese, as well as Samoan, Native Hawaiian, and other Pacific Islander groups—frequently come from low-income backgrounds and are first-generation college students. As such, they face similar barriers to enrolling and succeeding in college that other low-income and first-generation students face.

Statistics can also mask other challenges faced by Asian American/Pacific Islander students, including others' perceptions of them as "permanent foreigners" (Wu 2003). These perceptions can contribute to a negative campus climate and to feelings of isolation on the part of individual students. In addition to disaggregating data for more nuanced information about this diverse community, campuses should be mindful about offering safe spaces that affirm Asian American/Pacific Islander students' racial identities, self efficacy, and sense of belonging.

Myth #5:
We Can't Collect Data on Small Numbers of URM Students

Many CDI campuses had small numbers of URM students relative to their overall student populations, and very small numbers of American Indian/Alaska Native students, in particular. As a result, issues facing these students were often ignored by campus leaders. At times, low numbers of students also skewed quantitative data. The ERT helped campuses work through this quandary, noting that low numbers were a challenge for *quantitative* analyses but represented an excellent opportunity for deeper *qualitative* analyses—including focus groups and structured interviews—regarding American Indian/Alaska Native and other URM students' persistence, experience of the campus climate, and academic success. In addition, when CDI campuses had very small numbers of URM students from particular groups, leaders were advised to aggregate their quantitative data into a single URM group so that they could learn about any differences that might exist between URM students and other students.

Balancing Attention to Access with Attention to Success

As mentioned previously, many campuses focus on increasing the number of URM students (and faculty and staff) to attain compositional diversity and in the process may not pay as much attention to whether these students, faculty, and staff are successful. Several CDI campuses intensified outreach efforts in communities of color to increase the number of URM students enrolling on campus, but campus leaders often overlooked elements that impeded URM students' success once they were on campus. This was clearly counterproductive from the perspective of the broader goals of the CDI, as well as in terms of the amount of resources that went into outreach efforts that ultimately did not make an appreciable difference over time.

Gathering Systematic Accounts of URM and Low-Income Student Experiences

It is critical for campus leaders to look into ways to *systematically* gather data about the experiences of URM and low-income students in order to better match programs and services to their needs. At some CDI campuses, there was a tendency to appoint one or two URM or low-income students to diversity committees and then assume that their experiences reflected those of all URM and low-income students. Students also sometimes felt they could speak for their respective groups, and so campus leaders often relied on this strategy until the ERT pointed out that this approach led to "tokenizing" one or two students as the voices of a broad and diverse community.

In meetings with URM students on several campuses, ERT members encountered individuals who described great progress on their campuses but also disclosed negative incidents they had experienced personally. These students defended the institutions' efforts even in the face of negative incidents, often noting, "They're doing the best they can." They may have felt it would be disloyal to the people involved in the CDI—especially faculty and staff of color—to speak about negative incidents more publicly. Some students might not have been able to make the link between their individual negative experiences and an unsupportive campus culture. As a consequence, the ERT found that the picture of campus climate that was put forward by some of the colleges and universities may have been more positive, and less accurate, than was the actual case.

Systematically gathering data and appropriately using disaggregated satisfaction survey data, rather than relying on anecdotal comments from a few students, will help campus leaders develop a more accurate picture of how URM and low-income students are faring on campus. Such data should minimally include basic indicators of academic success (e.g., retention, GPA, persistence and success in specific majors, representation in honors programs). Ideally, data would also include evidence of preparation for the next level of education (e.g., preparing for graduate or professional school if attending a four-year institution, or transferring to a four-year institution if attending a community college), satisfaction and engagement with the campus environment (e.g., amount and quality of interactions with faculty, salience of programs and services), and preparation for work and leadership in a diverse society.

This systematic data collection should be both quantitative and qualitative in nature. Focus groups, regular interactions with identity/affinity groups, and input from a broad cross-section of individual students over time are some strategies that campuses can use to collect qualitative information about URM and low-income student experiences and avoid some of the pitfalls previously mentioned.

> **The Danger of Exclusionary Practices**
>
> One CDI campus committee uncovered data indicating that many students of color were dissatisfied with the climate at the institution. Administrators attributed this finding to the small numbers of students of color on campus and dismissed it because they felt that the dissatisfaction could only be addressed by increasing its compositional diversity. However, the committee later discovered that students of color were unhappy because they felt their views were marginalized. These feelings grew out of their absence on campus committees and the administration's failure to address the needs of their student organization. In this case, including previously discounted voices in campus decision making could have helped inform the process and could itself have served as a remedy for a "chilly" climate.

Understanding the Impetus behind Diversity Efforts

Diversity efforts can be affected by external forces as well as internal forces, and these forces can either propel diversity efforts forward or restrict them in some way. For example, a new grant from a private foundation would be an external force likely to boost efforts, while budget cuts would be an internal force likely to hamper efforts. Campus leaders typically develop or cut back on programs, services, and projects in response to these forces. This often leads to activities that exist either in isolation or in competition with one another.

Isolated activities, regardless of their effectiveness, rarely address the complexity of the forces at play or reflect the level of effort needed to implement comprehensive diversity work. To remedy this, campus leaders should first conduct an audit of existing forces related to diversity work and develop a coherent and campus-wide response to them. This also enables leaders to establish baseline data against which they can judge the effectiveness of later strategies and identify constituents who are calling for action, or pushing against action, and productively engage them in the work.

Recognizing and Compensating for Burn Out

The literature on diversity in higher education focuses a great deal on programmatic and curricular innovations, but spends relatively less time on the experiences of the people doing the work. One particular issue on many of the CDI campuses concerned individuals who withdrew from diversity work because they were not included in campus-wide planning efforts that could make a substantial difference in the quality of life at the institution. The ERT encountered numerous constituents who were "burned out," some because they participated in diversity work for years with little campus-wide change to show for their efforts, and some because they were never asked *how* the work could be improved. Most often these individuals were URM faculty and staff members. Many did not have official diversity-related positions or duties, but they had taken on grassroots work in diversity because of their desire to build more inclusive campuses.

The ERT listened to these individuals carefully in order to understand the reasons behind burnout. Some were frustrated because they were frequently sought out by URM students for advice and mentoring, but they were given no reward or recognition for this significant time commitment and the toll it took on their scholarly and professional pursuits. On the flip side, some were frustrated because when they tried to focus solely on their position responsibilities and remove themselves from diversity work, they were criticized by their communities for "selling out." These individuals noted that this "catch-22" situation was one that most white faculty and staff members did not have to face.

Additionally, URM faculty, staff, and students described the numerous times they were tapped to participate in campus-wide and departmental committees—some related to diversity, some not. While trying to ensure compositionally diverse committees was an important goal, very small numbers of URM constituents meant that a few people had to shoulder a very large burden. The situation grew even more frustrating during instances where URM committee members felt silenced by members of the group—they were even more painfully aware that their sole purpose seemed to be to "provide representation." A related frustration arose when URM committee members were the only members to voice concerns about diversity in the course of general committee meetings, or to voice concerns about race/ethnicity in the course of diversity committee meetings. They felt that white committee members were shirking their responsibility to keep race/ethnicity and other diversity issues "on the table" at these meetings.

The ERT advised campus leaders to collect stories of URM constituents' experiences in doing diversity work to begin to assess the disparity that might exist between URM and white constituents, the impact informal work had on URM constituents' professional duties, and the extent to which URM constituents felt they were able to create actual change. The ERT recognized that when the number of URM staff, faculty, and students is small to begin with, the loss associated with burnout can be especially devastating to campus efforts to create a diverse learning environment and inclusive climate.

Over the five-year span of the CDI, URM constituents mentioned many times that they felt they needed to "leave their culture at the door" when they engaged in their day-to-day work on campus. Many of them did not feel free to express their emotions and personal perspectives on issues, and multiple modes of expression, especially connected to culture and identity, were unintentionally silenced if not suppressed. On some campuses this silencing happened more often among faculty, staff, and administrators than among students. Many individuals reported that they simply made it through their work days, rather than contributing fully to the betterment of the campus.

Acknowledging Long-Term Advocates

Campus leaders can support and revitalize long-term advocates for diversity by publicly recognizing their accomplishments and underscoring the importance of their efforts in achieving the institution's mission. Some campuses present diversity awards at campus-wide recognition events, such as opening convocation or teaching, research, and service awards ceremonies. This places diversity efforts on par with other institutional objectives and also prevents the recognition from being a celebration by and for diversity advocates alone.

Chapter 4
Promising Practices

This chapter details a set of promising practices related to policies, programs, and planning for sustainability. They can also be categorized by the four dimensions of Smith's (1995) framework for diversity to help ensure that campus leaders take comprehensive action across all major areas of institutional functioning (see fig. 4).

Figure 4. Promising practices for undertaking comprehensive diversity work, by dimension

Institutional Viability and Vitality
- Link mission and goals for diversity
- Develop leadership throughout the institution
- Establish a chief diversity officer position
- Hire URM faculty and work to ensure their success
- Create a powerful story about the work

Education and Scholarship
- Build faculty and staff competencies to work with a compositionally diverse student body
- Leverage internal and external forces for change

Access and Success
- Strengthen connections with high schools and communities
- Increase transfer student presence on campus
- Coordinate URM graduate admissions across programs
- Focus on both race/ethnicity and income status
- Identify "unknown" students on campus
- Monitor GPA data by semester
- Move beyond basic success indicators
- Focus on gateway courses
- Institute high-achievement approaches across the curriculum
- Encourage URM and low-income students to pursue graduate studies

Campus Climate and Intergroup Relations
- Turn critical incidents into opportunities to improve campus climate and foster learning
- Develop effective lines of communication

These practices are referred to as "promising" because the ERT found that a number of elements affected the success of strategies campus leaders used to undertake comprehensive diversity work, including institutional type, mission, selectivity, structure, and aspirations; size and composition of the student body, faculty, and staff; location; resources; historical legacy of inclusion or exclusion; and academic and student cultures. Within the Campus Diversity Initiative, none of these elements consistently had a positive or negative impact on progress, but campus leaders had to attend to all or most of these elements and tailor practices accordingly in order to make progress. For example, leaders at a large research university found it difficult to sustain a campus-wide coordinating team because of institutional size and decentralized administrative structures, so they developed different mechanisms for coordinating efforts than the small liberal arts colleges in the project.

Furthermore, calling a practice "promising" recognizes that it is rarely the mere presence of a practice that makes it successful. The "how" matters greatly. This includes how a practice is introduced into the environment, how it is developed, how it is positioned within the institution, how it is evaluated, how seriously it is taken, and how it connects to broader goals. Given this, the ERT judged a practice to be promising if it:

- developed an institution-level perspective on diversity work;
- fostered cross-campus collaboration;
- was based on research (e.g., on diversity or evaluation);
- used data to indicate progress;
- established manageable and measurable action that could be sustained.

Campus leaders would benefit from carefully reviewing the entire set of practices detailed here and then determining, with a cross-section of their own campus constituents, what combination of practices would be most helpful given their institution's mission, history, and culture; goals for comprehensive diversity work; level of support and resistance to the work; and level and type of resources available.

Link Mission and Goals for Diversity

The ERT found that when an institution's mission explicitly connected to and reinforced a comprehensive approach to diversity, campus constituents were more likely to view diversity as part of the overall educational enterprise and less likely to see it strictly in terms of numbers of students, faculty, and staff or a narrow set of programs. Furthermore, a comprehensive notion of diversity was more likely to reach different constituents if it related to areas of campus practice that mattered to each group. For example, language in the mission that underscores the importance of a racially/ethnically diverse faculty to scholarly endeavors will likely motivate faculty in different ways than language that focuses solely on the need for URM faculty to serve as role models for students.

Ensure That Institutional Mission Includes Language on Diversity

All twenty-eight campuses had some reference to diversity within their mission statements at the start of the CDI, but some institutions used the CDI as an opportunity to strengthen the language that was in place. Some also developed diversity mission statements that would complement the broader mission and provide greater detail about the value of diversity.

Mission Statements and Diversity—Examples from CDI Campuses

"[The university] educates women and men for leadership and participation in a diverse society, and emphasizes generosity of spirit, compassion for the human condition, sensitivity to global interdependence, and enthusiasm for lifelong learning by its active engagement in the multiple communities it serves."

"[The university] educates students to . . . acquire the knowledge and skills necessary to effect thoughtful changes in a global, multicultural society."

"We educate leaders for a global society who are strong in character and judgment, confident in their identity and vocation, and committed to service and justice."

Broadening the Language of Mission Statements

Meacham and Barrett sought to determine how deeply diversity had become institutionalized in American higher education. These researchers reviewed the mission statements of campuses listed in the Princeton Review's 2002 version of *The Best 331 Colleges*. According to these authors, "mission statements represent a consensus on campus-wide values, expectations for student learning and development, and a statement of campus priorities for many years ahead" (2003, 5). They reviewed the Web sites of all 331 campuses for the institution's mission statement. If no mission statement was provided, they authors examined the institution's purpose, vision, goals or aims for students. They identified statements for 312 campuses. Within this group, 41 percent (n=129) included diversity as a descriptor for their students or as a goal for the composition of the student body, but only 27 percent (n= 85) included diversity as a student learning goal (student learning, in this study, collapsed both knowledge of and appreciation for diversity). This finding indicates that simply including diversity in campus statements is not enough. In many cases, the language used to describe diversity was narrowly focused on composition rather than connected to core educational goals for students and the institution's long-term viability and vitality.

Put Mission into Action with Regard to Diversity

Deep connections between mission and diversity work are necessary for success, but language attesting to the importance of diversity in the mission does not always translate into comprehensive action. The ERT found that when senior leaders understood diversity as being critical to institutional vitality, a campus was more successful in "living" its institutional mission and stated commitment to diversity.

Develop Leadership throughout the Institution

When a campus first undertakes comprehensive diversity work, it is wise to establish a team representing a cross-section of the institution to oversee implementation and evaluation efforts. This team should consist of faculty, students, and staff. At most of the CDI campuses, teams included senior faculty and administrators, student leaders, long-term diversity advocates, and the chief diversity officer when such a role existed. Toward the end of the CDI, a few campuses expanded their teams to include representatives from each school or key department. One CDI campus with a religious mission included the director of church relations on the committee, while another college with strong links to its graduates included recent alumni.

A broad-based team is critical to connect the work to the different constituents the team members represent. Often the best way to persuade individuals to join a broad-based effort is to couch the work in terms of their specific interests and to have the work introduced by someone who shares their role. For example, faculty members are likely to be interested in aspects of diversity work related to curriculum, pedagogy, research, and student learning, and another faculty member would be the best "ambassador" to help them get connected.

Yet this comprehensive, collaborative approach runs counter to how most institutions are currently organized.[1] It requires interaction among constituents across traditional organizational boundaries and perhaps a reenvisioning of how resources will be distributed in order to accomplish goals.

Departments and Units—Entry Points for Significant Change

Because much planning, decision making, and rewarding of efforts take place at the department or unit level within a campus, senior leaders need to ensure that diversity is regularly "on the agenda" at meetings of these mid-level leaders, much as budget and technology items are. Without the sustained involvement of deans, department chairs, and student affairs unit directors, an institution risks isolating both people and activities, and the successes, innovations, and wisdom that exist in particular locations will not be shared across campus.

---

1 For example, administrative and academic structures are typically divided up in ways that are operationally convenient, but not necessarily educationally effective or supportive, particularly for URM and low-income students. Traditional organizational boundaries often reflect a highly bureaucratic system as well as a faculty-driven, "collegial" system that favors isolation within the classroom as well as within research (Williams, Berger, and McClendon 2005). The result is that units and systems often operate on parallel tracks, or worse, in competition with one another. Reward systems, too, often fail to recognize (and even penalize) individuals who cross boundaries.

> **A Note about Senior Leadership**
>
> For institutions to achieve success with comprehensive diversity work, senior leaders should have a strong understanding of the issues, support an institution-wide approach, directly engage with the work on a regular basis, request frequent progress reports based on a set of indicators, and act on these reports. This communicates to constituents and the larger public the importance of diversity as a core institutional value and central component of institutional viability and vitality. And while not all senior leaders may champion this work from the outset, discussions of diversity that link it to institutional mission, educational excellence, and institutional viability may help build support for this work over time.

Establish a Chief Diversity Officer Position

Because diversity efforts span all areas and functions of an institution, an important element for success is to have a mechanism to coordinate the work and its evaluation and to identify where greater synergy might take place among various elements. Developing a senior-level position focused on diversity that has access to core institutional decision makers is one way to provide both coordination and depth in sustaining diversity efforts. This position is referred to here as a chief diversity officer (Williams and Wade-Golden 2006).

Establishing a chief diversity officer position is a promising practice when the roles and responsibilities for the position are well defined, and when the position provides the individual with some authority to hold constituents accountable for progress. The chief diversity officer should also have the authority to put in place a timely and effective monitoring process, including a regular review of data on student access and success that have been disaggregated by race/ethnicity, gender, income level, and other factors the institution feels are important to its overall goals for diversity. He or she should involve a broad cross-section of constituents in the work and coordinate their efforts.

> **The Chief Diversity Officer—Elements of Success**
>
> The chief diversity officer will more likely advance comprehensive diversity work when he or she
>
> - helps connect this work to mission and core institutional values;
> - understands his or her role on behalf of the institution;
> - recognizes that organizational learning is key to improving institutional culture and practices;
> - motivates people beyond mandates and compliance to see how their efforts contribute to institution-level goals;
> - oversees the integration of efforts across campus and at all levels;
> - creates synergy between elements of the work so that it advances in rich and perhaps unanticipated ways;
> - instills a strong sense of shared ownership and responsibility for the outcomes of the diversity initiative.

Hire URM Faculty—and Work to Ensure Their Success

Both the ERT and the campuses recognized that increasing the presence of URM faculty would contribute to both goals of the CDI.[2] More than half of the CDI campuses made URM faculty hiring a strategic priority. However, as the findings noted earlier, many of the campuses experienced significant turnover, which dampened the success some had in increasing their numbers of URM hires. The ERT learned the following powerful lessons from these experiences.

Link Hiring to Institutional Priorities, Planning, and Leadership

The ERT found that there was a greater likelihood of sustained change over time when faculty hiring efforts were linked to institutional priorities, planning, and leadership. In such cases, campus leaders saw faculty hiring as central not only to building institutional capacity to engage diversity in governance, curriculum development, research, and advising, but also to building credibility with broader communities. These leaders understood that the institution's attractiveness—to students and faculty alike—was in part dependent on the compositional diversity of the faculty.

On the more successful campuses, leaders also helped existing faculty understand the link between searches and larger institutional purposes and priorities. These leaders recognized and respected faculty autonomy at the "local" level of the departments and search committees, but they also linked these processes to campus-wide imperatives and incentives—for example, by creating pools of money to bring more final candidates to campus.

> ### Sparking Interest in Faculty Careers
>
> Several of the CDI campuses worked to increase access and success for URM graduate students. Strategies often centered on providing fellowships, yet these alone were not sufficient. Substantive programmatic efforts—linking URM and low-income graduate students to each other, to faculty, and to shared intellectual work—helped to create a supportive environment and contributed to URM graduate students' interest in, and success in, pursuing faculty careers.

Learn from the Experiences of Current and Former URM Faculty

Because prevailing perceptions about URM candidates ("there aren't any," "they wouldn't want to come here," "we can't afford them") provide excuses for failure, it was helpful for campus leaders to understand why and through what networks current URM faculty came to their institutions. These faculty members served to debunk existing myths and provided valuable information about specific elements that attracted them to the campus.

---

2 For example, researchers have found that faculty of color and women faculty are more likely than their white and male counterparts to include issues related to diversity in their courses and research and use active-learning and student-centered pedagogies in the classroom (Astin et al. 1997; Milem 1999).

Likewise, campus leaders realized that conducting exit interviews with URM faculty who were leaving, along with other methods to investigate how the environment influenced URM faculty success, yielded important information. Some campuses also found it helpful to incorporate mechanisms for URM faculty success—mentoring programs, detailed information about promotion and retention, and clear expectations about duties and responsibilities—into hiring plans and agreements.

Create a Climate of Shared Commitment and Responsibility

Senior leaders, department chairs, and existing faculty all had key roles to play in efforts to increase the presence of URM faculty, and on more successful campuses, these roles included early and continuous involvement. Campuses were more successful when chairs and faculty viewed these efforts as essential for strengthening their departments, both on campus and nationally. Finally, when an institutional commitment for diversity was reflected in the "language" of the campus—in the mission and goals, on the Web site, and in the strategic plan and other statements of academic purpose—it communicated to applicants that the campus might be serious about diversifying the faculty.

Less successful campuses discovered that simple pronouncements that "diversity must be increased" were insufficient and that waiting until a final list of candidates was developed was too late. When these efforts were viewed as optional or someone else's concern, the prevailing perceptions about URM faculty hiring often provided a rationale for a lack of success.

Tackling URM Faculty Turnover

As mentioned earlier, overall faculty demographics at the CDI campuses were not changing as fast as the rates of new hiring might have suggested. Members of the ERT developed a turnover quotient (TQ) to show the degree to which new URM hires were adding to faculty compositional diversity or simply replacing URM faculty who had left.

Campus data are not always collected in ways that can show institutional progress over time. The turnover quotient (TQ) should prove helpful in doing this. The TQ focuses on turnover for URM faculty, but it can be applied to any subgroup. The quotient is expressed as follows:

$$TQ = [1 - (\frac{EndPeriodURMFac - StartPeriodURMFac}{NewURMHires})] \times 100$$

The overall effort of diversifying the faculty at CDI campuses depended on where an institution began, the rate of hiring, the level of diversity among new hires, and the degree of turnover. The data suggested that there was a "revolving door" that undermined campuses' ability to make significant changes in their overall faculty demographics. Campuses need to pay close attention to this revolving door if they expect to actually diversify their faculty. Setting benchmarks can help focus attention as well as measure progress. For more information, see the related brief, *The Revolving Door for Underrepresented Minority Faculty in Higher Education* (Moreno et al. 2006a), available at www.irvine.org/assets/pdf/pubs/education/insight_Revolving_Door.pdf.

Create a Powerful Story about the Work

Over the course of the project, communication proved to be critical in advancing institutional goals for diversity and facilitating organizational learning. The CDI campus teams were encouraged to utilize their six-month reports to create a powerful story about the work and share information with other constituents in order to improve their efforts. Indeed, when teams developed reports to serve the campus rather than the foundation, they moved from grant compliance mode to learning mode. They not only intended for a wider audience to have access to the data, but also expected to obtain broader feedback to guide change. Key elements in the communication process involve (1) who shapes the story of diversity on campus, (2) who tells the story, (3) who hears the story, and (4) who validates (gives feedback about) the story.

Who Shapes the Story

The effectiveness of the story was influenced by who called for the story to be told. When this person (or persons) possessed a high level of knowledge about diversity and some amount of authority, the story gained credibility. Reports that were guided by the collaborative efforts of an active committee benefited from being shaped by a broader and sometimes divergent set of perspectives. Likewise, it was important to have a broad base of constituents weigh in on the structure and content of the report as part of the process. When participants from across campus (students, faculty, staff, and administrators) and from external communities influenced how data were interpreted and used for organizational learning, this enriched the story.

Who Tells the Story

Depending on who told the story, the perception of it changed. On some CDI campuses, senior administrators of color were, at times, cast as "diversity experts" regardless of their expertise or position. Such situations were problematic in that they presumed that any person of color would be an expert in diversity work, rejected the experience and expertise of other campus constituents, isolated "ownership" of the initiative to a few people, and risked arousing suspicion about the initiative because ownership was not broad-based.

On some of the campuses, development and advancement staff members drafted required reports for the foundation. However, that often resulted in documents that highlighted successes rather than organizational learning, which would include missteps and failures. Neglect of pressing issues and barriers limited the campuses' ability to learn from their data collection efforts. However, with input from other campus constituents, development and advancement staff came to play a key role in telling the story of progress and describing the challenges faced in achieving comprehensive goals for diversity. Furthermore, more successful CDI campuses often had institutional research staff play a role beyond collecting and "crunching" data. Their interpretation of data also contributed to telling the story of progress and challenges.

Regardless of who told the story, both the clarity about diversity and campus engagement with diversity were enhanced when story tellers used data to communicate the story of progress (or lack thereof) to the larger campus.

Who Hears the Story

Within the CDI, several issues arose that prevented a broad group from hearing about progress—the setbacks as well as the successes. On some campuses, teams did not share data openly out of concern about negative information and lack of progress. Some teams lacked a process and an infrastructure to analyze information and make it broadly accessible. The ERT also discovered efforts, at times, to suppress information by those responsible for aspects of the work, due to fear that a lack of progress would reflect badly on their professional standing.

Who Validates the Story

Some campus teams found it difficult to structure a "feedback loop" where different constituents could react to data analyses and translate them into individual and institutional action. Many of the CDI campus teams struggled to develop an effective system for two-way communication. Open forums, for example, provided opportunities for multiple constituencies to give feedback, but systems to capture and process the feedback were often not in place. Efforts to disseminate findings or process constituent feedback that were perceived to be disingenuous ultimately hindered campus goals for diversity.

> **From Presentation to Dialogue**
>
> Constituents will provide different interpretations of findings based on their location within the institution and the perspectives they bring to the work, and it is important that data presentations leave room for genuine dialogue about differences in interpretation and meaning making. It is especially important to create a context where individuals can talk openly and honestly about campus dynamics, particularly if senior leaders are in the room.

Build Faculty and Staff Competencies to Work with a Compositionally Diverse Student Body

The ERT observed many instances where faculty and staff clearly did not possess the knowledge, skills, or experience to help improve college access and success for URM and low-income students. It is particularly important that campus leaders ascertain the needs of different constituent groups—faculty, staff, students, mid-level administrators, and upper-level administrators—in order for them to be competent to work with a compositionally diverse student body. Leaders should look to their own diversity and evaluation experts as sources for knowledge and realize that constituents need time to incorporate new knowledge and be socialized to new tasks.

Over many years, the ERT observed instances where people were expected to fundamentally change their roles and responsibilities but did not understand the purpose and design of the new work that campus leaders expected of them. Creating a more welcoming environment for URM and low-income students requires new knowledge and skills in fostering their success and in developing an institution-wide perspective on the work to be done.

Within the CDI, several actions helped faculty and staff develop these competencies. The actions included establishing teams for learning and action; securing time away from campus—or at least dedicated time on campus—for reflection, learning, and planning; and being strategic about the kinds of learning that would most increase constituents' ability to do the new work.

Create Core Teams

Having teams—versus individuals—develop and oversee the implementation and evaluation of comprehensive diversity work contributes to professional development. This strategy can be particularly useful for collecting and analyzing data and ensuring that the results are broadly shared. Staff, faculty, administrators, and students on several CDI campuses benefited from experiences that allowed them to work with data and grasp the meaning behind data.

The annual CDI evaluation seminars and national diversity conferences brought these core teams of campus constituents together to discuss progress, setbacks, and questions and to learn about strategies that other campuses used in undertaking comprehensive diversity work. During these gatherings, participants heard about new research, programs, and methods to enhance communication and identify potential collaborators.

Provide Time Away

When teams had time away from campus, members were able to map out what needed to be done to be successful, reflect upon their campus diversity goals, and develop plans to get the work done. The ERT helped teams use the off-campus time to enhance their work by making the development of concrete action plans part of the structure of the gatherings.

Build Constituents' Capacity To Do the Work

The ERT advised teams to select professional development activities that would intentionally increase constituents' capacity to accomplish the new tasks they were confronting. For example, the ERT helped guide the CDI teams' learning at national conferences by highlighting sessions that would likely deepen their understanding of the educational benefits of diversity and enhance their evaluation work. The teams were also able to interact with representatives from the Western Association of Schools and Colleges at the evaluation seminars. This allowed the teams to place their CDI evaluation in a larger context of educational quality and realize the points of overlap between their efforts and accreditation review processes. These conversations helped team members feel confident that they would be able to conduct manageable yet robust evaluation and use the results to advance their institutional goals. These connections also increased the likelihood that the CDI campuses would sustain their efforts beyond the external grants.

Leverage Internal and External Forces for Change

It is important for campuses to balance internal and external forces that influence diversity work. As campus leaders strive to increase access and success for URM and low-income students and build campus capacity for overall diversity efforts in ways that promote organizational learning, they must develop institutional structures to support actions and to monitor progress. Using an inclusive approach and keeping it focused on the institution's educational mission will help foster shared responsibility toward goals and minimize oppositional forces.

Establish Clear Roles for Schools and Departments

A strong sense of shared responsibility for sustaining diversity efforts can itself be a dynamic internal force. This is especially critical for graduate program admissions and faculty hiring because the typically decentralized nature of these processes can impede progress. As campus constituents document the impact of their efforts, it is likely that more schools and departments will want to contribute. Contributions may include curricular enhancements, professional development opportunities to learn new pedagogies, or new community connections that can lead to increased faculty and student participation in service learning. Rewards can also help increase "demand" to do this work. For example, re-granting programs designed to develop new courses, scholarship, or faculty–student research projects on diversity issues can greatly expand the number of faculty and students who can engage in such activities. Although such programs may originate at the institutional level, they can be incorporated into schools and departments to help create a shared expectation for faculty, staff, and students to undertake this work.

Establish Clear Roles for Senior Leaders

National, regional, and local conditions influence campus diversity work. As noted earlier, anti-affirmative action litigation has pushed many campuses into "compliance mode." While some campus leaders have responded to these influences by abandoning race-conscious programs, others have continued to address diversity proactively and intentionally while complying with the law. These leaders have recognized that it is their role to examine internal and external influences on diversity efforts, address these influences strategically and for organizational learning, and strive to act in accordance with the institution's core educational mission.

Strengthen Connections with High Schools and Communities

The more successful CDI campuses were strategic in connecting with high schools and communities previously neglected in outreach efforts. Significantly, this practice yielded success in terms of URM student access regardless of campus selectivity. Critical factors included

- having admissions staff members who were from—or at least familiar with and comfortable working in—these communities, and who found ways to connect with students even when access to high school counselors was limited or unavailable;
- building relationships with high school students through summer programs and throughout the senior year of high school (or earlier years), and linking these programs to ongoing processes and activities such as admissions and financial aid workshops;
- having a racially/ethnically diverse campus, which can make a campus more attractive to students and speaks to the integrity of campus statements about diversity.

> **Build Inclusive Admissions Practices**
>
> During one site visit, the ERT liaison made a point of asking about data that indicated low enrollment of African American students, given the institution's geographic location near several African American communities. The admissions director acknowledged that the institution's admissions criteria and review process may have been unnecessarily limiting the pool of African American students. Admissions criteria included SAT scores, high school grade point average, and in many programs, samples of student work. The review process involved only a small group of campus constituents. This site visit discussion prompted the campus to use a broader set of admissions criteria and include more members of the campus community in the review process. (For more information on broadening admissions criteria, see Sedlacek 2004 and Bial 2004.)

Increase Transfer Student Presence on Campus

A sizeable number of URM and low-income students begin their postsecondary careers at community colleges. The more successful CDI campuses developed partnerships with these institutions as a key strategy to increase URM student access to four-year colleges.

Coordinate URM Graduate Admissions across Programs

Graduate admissions are decentralized processes at most master's and doctorate degree–granting campuses, and because of this, an institution-wide goal of increasing the presence of URM graduate students requires coordination among various programs. Several CDI campuses had begun this coordination process, which included discussions among campus leaders about ways to identify potential talent beyond the traditional indicators of academic potential. Leaders at some of the CDI doctorate degree–granting institutions began to understand that their practices would influence the nation's pool of future faculty. They also realized that given the significant racial/ethnic diversity among undergraduate students in California, there was great potential to help diversify the graduate student—and thus faculty—pool.

With this in mind, one CDI campus linked its fellowships to the students rather than to the departments. This enabled students to engage in interdisciplinary studies across departments and allowed them to move within the institution as their research interests evolved. Such approaches, however, mean that campus leaders may need to address institutional cultures that work against interdisciplinary work.

Focus on Both Race/Ethnicity and Income Level

The ERT worked with campuses to evaluate their progress on increasing access and success for URM and low-income students. Because these two groups overlap, the ERT wanted to better assess both the economic diversity among URM students and the racial/ethnic diversity among low-income students. Even given the cautions about using Pell Grant data as an indicator of low-income status, it was clear from analyses of CDI campus data that income intersected with race/ethnicity in important ways (Moreno et al. 2006b).

Campus leaders will benefit from using their own financial aid eligibility and need-based awards data along with Pell Grant data to investigate the status of access and success for low-income students and to better understand the intersection of income and race/ethnicity as well as factors such as gender. Collecting such data provides campus leaders with more complete information about their students and this, in turn, can help shape resource allocation and student support services.

Identify "Unknown" Students on Campus

Several of the CDI campuses found that the percentage of "unknown" students increased substantially during the course of the project. This made it difficult for campus leaders to have an accurate understanding of the racial/ethnic demographics of the student population, which in turn made monitoring progress on access and success difficult.

Identifying "Unknown" Students—One Method

Over the course of several decades of working with campuses to establish diversity initiatives, the ERT encountered many people who assume that most, if not all, students who fall into the race/ethnicity "unknown" category are multiracial. As part of the CDI, members of the ERT analyzed admissions data alongside a second data source in which students identified their racial/ethnic identity post-enrollment. While there was variation among the three campuses in the study, overall, the results suggest that a sizeable portion of students in the unknown category are white, in addition to multiracial students who selected white as one of their categories. In the related brief (Smith et al. 2005), the authors offer five recommendations::

1. Collect racial/ethnic demographic data post-enrollment to identify unknown students.
2. Set campus-wide internal standards for using and reporting data.
3. Use consistent racial/ethnic categories across data sets.
4. Define all levels of racial/ethnic groupings (e.g., "students of color").
5. Provide details on the groups that constitute biracial and multiracial identities.

Monitor GPA Data by Semester

Campus leaders should review disaggregated GPA data in order to have a sense of how different groups of students are faring academically and to intervene if needed. Cumulative GPA data can provide some insight into student success, but semester-by-semester GPA data often prove more useful in terms of discovering *when* gaps between groups are established and whether specific interventions are helping students make gains. Similarly, campuses with graduate programs can monitor graduate student success by reviewing disaggregated GPA data on a semester-by-semester basis, as well as data on graduation, time to degree by program, and thesis versus non-thesis options.

Move beyond Basic Success Indicators

Determining whether students have achieved key learning outcomes requires more sophisticated direct measures of learning (Miller and Leskes 2005). New measures of learning have begun to move beyond basic success indicators, such as standardized test scores and GPA, enabling campus leaders to document student learning in ways that can demonstrate institution-level progress (Hersh 2005). Course-embedded assessments, rubrics that help faculty gauge students' knowledge as they progress through their majors, and e-portfolios that document learning cumulatively over time and across curricular and cocurricular activities are some of the emerging methods (Leskes and Miller 2006; Miller and Leskes 2005).

Focus on Gateway Courses

Examining data on gateway courses, especially in the STEM fields, is an important way to identify gaps in student success.[3] These data should comprise several years' worth of grade distributions in gateway courses, disaggregated by race/ethnicity, income level, and other pertinent criteria. On some campuses, the presence of achievement gaps among different groups of students has led to course reorganization, including greater use of active pedagogies. At a few of the CDI campuses, faculty members resisted the notion of reorganizing, believing this would lower standards. Yet departments that restructured gateway courses to focus on high achievement for all students proved this assumption false.[4]

Institute "High Achievement" Approaches across the Curriculum

Setting high expectations for students has a positive effect on both retention and success throughout their educational careers (Comer 2004; Hrabowski 2004; Steele 2003). The ERT found that CDI campuses increased the effectiveness of their bridge programs when leaders shifted focus from assumptions about participants' "high risk" to the social capital, knowl-

---

[3] Gateway courses serve as entry-level requirements for majors. For example, calculus is a gateway course for engineering, physics, and mathematics.

[4] Campus leaders could "ratchet up" this practice by also paying close attention to entire disciplines (e.g., STEM) where URM and low-income student success is often disproportionately low.

edge, and abilities that participants bring to college.[5] Programs that tapped this capital through course redesign and new pedagogies helped accelerate participants' learning.[6]

This culture of high expectations can continue to be fostered in the first year through honors-style programs, such as learning communities or other types of clustered courses that bring groups of students together and connect them with senior faculty in small, discussion-based settings. These programs might focus on topics or themes that are relevant to the lives and experiences of URM and low-income students in order to foster greater connection between the students and their academic pursuits. Beyond the first year, the culture of high expectations can be continued through undergraduate research opportunities, where URM and low-income students engage one-on-one or in small groups with faculty in discovery work.

It is essential for campus leaders to institute faculty development programs where faculty members can learn these new pedagogical approaches as well as techniques to support URM and low-income students. Campus leaders should also work to develop collaboration across units that support URM and low-income student success throughout the curriculum and cocurricular programs. Collaboration is particularly important between student affairs and academic affairs, among student groups, between student groups and other campus constituents, and among departments. When done well, such collaboration can help maximize resources to ensure URM and low-income student success, specifically, and all students' success, generally.

Encourage URM and Low-Income Students to Pursue Graduate Studies

Another important element in creating high expectations is to encourage URM and low-income undergraduate students early on to aim for graduate and professional education. This entails providing them with "insider" views of such educational options, connecting them with current URM and low-income graduate students, and linking them to research and internship opportunities that will help prepare them for success in their later studies.

One CDI project focused partly on enhancing scholarship about race and ethnicity. The project linked faculty conducting research in these areas with graduate students—often but not always URM faculty as well as URM graduate students. The project also linked graduate students with URM undergraduates, which stimulated the latter students' interest in the discipline and in pursuing graduate studies.

For Campuses with Graduate Programs

Increasing the pipeline to graduate school also has the longer-term benefit of helping to diversify the faculty. Leaders on campuses with graduate programs should consider implementing activities that will help their own URM and low-income undergraduate students move successfully into these programs.

---

5 Bridge programs for admitted students typically take place during the summer between high school and college and can focus on academic preparation, social preparation, or both.

6 One CDI campus was successful in using a high-achievement approach with a longer bridge program in the STEM fields. This program began in middle school and extended into the summer between the freshman and sophomore years in college.

Turn Critical Incidents into Opportunities to Improve Campus Climate and Learning

Institutions often launch diversity initiatives and programs in response to critical events occurring on campus or in the larger society, such as a series of incidents involving racial/ethnic bias. One consequence of programming in *response* to incidents is that once the programs take place, urgency sometimes recedes and the campus returns to "business as usual." This form of crisis management has a detrimental effect on the kind of comprehensive diversity work discussed in these pages, and it is damaging to the campus climate generally. Initiatives and programs that leaders develop following negative incidents should provide opportunities to foster student learning and should make a broader impact across campus.

Develop Effective Lines of Communication

When campus leaders effectively communicate the goals, strategies, and expected outcomes for diversity across campus and engender dialogue about them, constituents have the opportunity to share diverse (and sometimes divergent) views. Taking multiple viewpoints into consideration facilitates the development of a shared perspective and minimizes the growth of oppositional forces on campus.

Many campuses held open forums in order to communicate information about the CDI to students, faculty, and staff and to receive feedback from them. Such forums generally began as a presentation of the views of at least two sides—promoters and skeptics—followed by a discussion about outcomes and strategies to achieve outcomes. A series of forums may be necessary to reach a point where dialogue becomes ongoing and useful in advancing the work.

Several CDI campuses complemented the general forums with meetings of smaller groups of constituents. These included informal lunch meetings with faculty, staff, and administrators; faculty–student meetings after classes; and more formal, ongoing interactions with groups such as the student government, faculty senate, president's cabinet, and key staff committees. It is important that such multi-level organizational interactions occur regularly to maintain the engagement of these constituents and open lines of communication. The regular exchange of information facilitates mid-course corrections to action as well as organizational learning.

Surveying campus constituents is another important communication strategy that can aid organizational learning. Surveys can measure faculty, staff, and student views of campus climate, intergroup relations, student learning and engagement, curriculum, and satisfaction with the institutional environment. Surveys of recent graduates can also help guide campus action by adding this group's perceptions of their experiences while in college. As noted elsewhere, information from such surveys is only useful when it is disaggregated by race/ethnicity, income level, and other pertinent factors.

Chapter 5
A Guide to Comprehensive Diversity Work

The previous chapters have described the story of the Campus Diversity Initiative, related quantitative and qualitative findings, and promising practices to help institutions build and sustain successful efforts. Drawing on the experience of the CDI as well as the broader experiences of the ERT, this chapter offers a step-by-step guide to developing and implementing comprehensive diversity work, using an organizational learning approach that is built on evaluation. As stated at the outset of this monograph, an organizational learning approach increases the likelihood that a campus will achieve and sustain institution-wide goals for diversity. These steps reflect the goals of the CDI—increasing access and success for URM and low-income students and building campus capacity to enhance and evaluate overall diversity efforts in ways that promoted organizational learning—and cover four areas:

- *Envisioning diversity efforts in relation to institutional mission.* A broad-based committee reviews and reflects on past diversity efforts—related to institutional viability, access and success, education and scholarship, and campus climate—in order to envision the "next generation" of comprehensive diversity work that reflects institutional mission.
- *Developing both campus-wide goals for diversity and strategies that are linked to institutional mission.* The committee uses a framework for diversity, with indicators, to create a set of measurable goals and strategies that are linked to institutional mission and values.
- *Generating and implementing an action plan to achieve goals and an evaluation plan to monitor progress.* The committee involves a wider set of constituents to outline goals and carry out strategies. The committee also sets up a manageable, evidenced-based evaluation plan where constituents monitor the strategies and processes being used, gather data to demonstrate whether progress is being made, and use results for educational improvement and organizational learning.
- *Establishing infrastructure to sustain organizational learning and meet evolving goals for diversity.* The committee identifies specific curricular and cocurricular actions, administrative units, and individuals needed to support goals, strategies, and evaluation in the future. This is done to ensure that diversity is integral to the institution's day-to-day functioning and that evolving goals for diversity are met.

> **Chart a Path for Future Success**
>
> At one CDI institution, campus leaders charged an individual with systematically compiling information about previous diversity work so that the leaders could begin charting future directions. This individual collected information from a broad group of constituents, summarized the findings, and validated this document with the campus leaders. The institution's next generation of work grew out of discussions of this document and centered on a particular aspect of mission related to graduate education. A broad group of constituents agreed on a plan of action, which entailed (1) engaging every member of the campus academic center that was to oversee the specific project to increase the number of graduate students of color, and (2) linking that work with larger institutional efforts to increase the number of URM faculty. The campus also hired a capable leader to guide and monitor URM faculty hiring and retention efforts. Over the course of the initiative, the campus had established a process of monitoring URM faculty hiring in each of its schools and colleges using the turnover quotient developed by the ERT.

1. Establish a Broad-Based Committee to Oversee the Work and Networks to Carry It Out

Establishing a broad-based committee is a crucial first step in engendering widespread responsibility and accountability for comprehensive diversity work. The presence of people with different vantage points allows for multiple perspectives to enter into the process and can help the group better recognize various internal and external forces for change. Campus leaders can conserve resources and create synergy with other efforts by utilizing existing committee structures, but regardless, the group should include

- senior-level decision makers, including senior admissions, academic affairs, and student affairs officers;
- academic deans and faculty members with expertise in diversity and evaluation;
- student leaders, especially those with experience in diversity work;
- the chief diversity officer and institutional research officer, where such positions exist.

The group should have strong inroads into decision-making processes, both through its membership and its reporting line. Because of the particular focus of this work on URM and low-income student access and success, campus leaders should ensure that the committee includes several students from these groups and that there is overall compositional diversity.

From the start, the committee should consider how it can involve additional constituents in the work. This will help connect a broader group of people to the work and protect the institution from the negative effects of transitions and turnover. Campus leaders can help constituents share a larger vision of diversity and prevent diversity work from becoming localized or isolated. Moreover, when the process is inclusive and different constituent groups are engaged, there is less chance for diversity efforts to become marginalized as other issues come into focus.

Committee, Know Thyself

Whether the committee is newly appointed or pre-existing, the group must recognize that some members may be new to diversity work. Others may have a long history with diversity efforts but be new to using an institution-wide approach. Many committee members may be unfamiliar with evaluation and monitoring processes. Those in charge of appointing the committee should ascertain what skills, experiences, and knowledge areas members can contribute to the work, and the committee members should share this information with each other. It is also important that the committee take the time needed to build cohesion and trust among members as well as to understand and incorporate the experiences and perspectives that members bring to the work. If a review of past diversity work has not already been undertaken, the committee should identify a means for gathering information about such efforts so as to avoid "reinventing the wheel" when developing future plans. The review and planning documents can also help socialize new members of the committee to the work ahead.

Tailor the Committee to Institutional Size

Institutional size has a strong influence on campus mission, and so it will also play a large role in how comprehensive diversity work will unfold on a campus. Campus leaders should consider this context carefully when deciding on the best structure and composition for the campus-wide committee. For instance, large institutions with many schools and colleges may want to adopt a two-tiered structure—where smaller, unit-specific committees are connected to a larger, university-wide committee. Several CDI campuses ultimately moved to this two-tier approach after beginning their efforts within a particular sub-section of the university. The unit-specific committees developed goals and strategies that were tailored to each college's or school's area of focus (e.g., law, education, arts and sciences). The university-wide committee made sure that various efforts connected to the institution's mission and goals for diversity and achieved coherence across units.

2. Review Past Efforts and Envision "Next Steps" in Relation to Institutional Mission

Committee members should examine the campus's previous diversity efforts in the context of institutional mission and, where needed, identify ways to establish stronger links between diversity work and mission. Linking the two will help ensure that diversity work has integrity and is taken seriously by various campus constituents.

The ERT is aware of campuses that have established diversity committees within boards of trustees. Given their fiduciary responsibilities, trustees who are members of a diversity committee can be powerful advocates for comprehensive campus efforts when they understand the critical link between diversity and institutional viability and vitality. They can also play a role in helping other trustees, and the general public, understand this important link.

3. Develop Institution-level Goals for Diversity That Are Linked to Mission

The committee should begin with a discussion about what it hopes to accomplish with its comprehensive diversity work and why. Five questions can help focus the committee's conversation.

1. *What are the challenges that our institution faces that require altering the status quo?* The committee would be wise to use a framework, such as the one developed by Smith (1995), to identify specific challenges across different areas of institutional functioning.
2. *Why is it important for our institution to undertake a comprehensive diversity effort to address these challenges?* This establishes a common understanding about why it is critical to do the work with an institution-level approach.
3. *What strategies can we use to address these challenges?* Strategies can be drawn from the research literature, from promising practices of peer institutions, or from previous campus action. This brainstorming process should generate as many ideas as possible.
4. *Which of the identified actions are manageable for the committee to pursue?* To answer this question, the committee should audit what the campus is already doing in comparison to what it wants to accomplish and examine the gap between current work and aspirations. The committee should also audit internal and external resources that may be available to undertake comprehensive diversity work, including people's time and expertise, materials and facilities, and financial resources. Committee members will not necessarily know about all potential sources of support, so they should include institutional advancement staff in this process.
5. *What will the institution accomplish as a result of this work?* The answer to this question becomes a goal to guide campus action. From a set of goals, the committee can draft a plan of action and a plan for evaluation.

> **Move Past the Plateau**
>
> Many campuses will enter the goal-setting process already having done some work on diversity, often in the areas of student compositional diversity, cultural programming, or a diversity requirement in the curriculum. These institutions often have difficulty figuring out strategic next steps beyond *people and programs*. Campus leaders need to push themselves and others to envision what *structures, policies, and rewards* would help embed diversity efforts more broadly and deeply into institutional planning, campus culture, and day-to-day work.

4. Design Strategies to Meet Goals

As the committee begins to develop strategies for achieving institutional goals for diversity, members may want to approach the task from their individual vantage points. For example, a faculty member in the biological sciences may want to develop strategies to enhance the success of URM students majoring in her field. An administrator with broader responsibilities may want to focus on strategies to increase URM student retention more generally. A student leader may want to devise strategies to increase student-led programming around diversity.

The next step is to reach consensus on a set of strategies that can be monitored for progress, and here too, committee members can bring their individual interests and expertise to bear on the actions. For example, should the lack of URM students in STEM fields emerge as a priority for the group, the biology faculty member may be best suited to lead an outreach effort where URM students in biology general education courses are introduced to the major. Other STEM faculty may develop resources to integrate diversity issues into existing courses or undertake new research on the ways in which diversity can deepen students' learning.

In the end, it is important that the committee creates a set of strategies that span the different areas of campus functioning—using the diversity framework in this task, as in goal-setting, is helpful. Strategies can build on previous efforts, expanding or amending them so that they will have increased impact, or they may be adapted from practices that have been successful on other campuses.

5. Generate an Action Plan to Enact Strategies and an Evaluation Plan to Monitor Progress

The mission-driven vision for the diversity work, the comprehensive goals, and the associated strategies serve as the foundation for developing campus action and evaluation plans. A detailed action plan serves as a guide to enact the strategies and ensure that tasks related to the strategies are completed in a timely way.

An evaluation plan should chart how the committee and other constituents will know they are making progress. The ERT provided the CDI campuses with a template (see appendix 3) to help them create their evaluation plans. Committee members can use the template to identify the goals, strategies, and expected outcomes of comprehensive diversity work. While the template does not specifically address the resources needed to undertake an initiative, identifying adequate resources is critical at this stage of the planning.

Committee members can then use the template to list measures of progress that will be appropriate given the campus context and the nature of the work to be done. The committee must also consider the instruments and collection mechanisms that will systematically capture the data needed to monitor progress. These collection mechanisms work best if the evaluation includes gathering baseline data, establishing benchmarks and timelines for data collection and analysis, and designating a set of individuals and units to oversee the process.[1]

Completing the evaluation template may lead committee members to revisit the campus goals and the means for achieving them. This is to be expected, and goals and strategies will shift over time as the committee and other constituents learn more about what elements help or hinder success.

> ### Do Away with Business as Usual
>
> Early in the CDI, many campus leaders responded to the James Irvine Foundation's call for institution-wide efforts and an organizational learning approach with familiar—and narrow—goals and strategies. These leaders wanted to create new programs that simply repeated what had been done previously, especially with regard to recruiting and retaining URM students. Likewise, many early evaluation plans were based on satisfaction surveys because of campus leaders' familiarity with them and because of the ease of administration. The campus leaders needed to go through several iterations of goals, strategies, action plans, and evaluation plans before they were able to move beyond "business as usual" and develop institution-level work. Overall, campuses experienced greater success when leaders focused as much energy on learning from past and current work as they had on securing external grants for their work.

6. Use Data to Monitor Progress, Make Adjustments and Mid-course Corrections, and Learn about "What Works"

Accurate and useable data are necessary for strategic decision making, and good data are fundamental to organizational learning. Without data, it would be extremely difficult to determine objectively whether progress is being made toward institutional goals. Like a financial audit, data collection and analysis around goals for diversity gives leaders an indication of the institution's solvency and well-being. Regular data collection and analysis over time help constituents understand the results of their actions in both the short term and long term.

The most effective evaluation process begins with the establishment of baseline data, which can be compared to later data sets for evidence of progress. The ERT devised a workbook to help guide institutions' data-collection processes. Each campus used the data to inform their decisions and to make adjustments and mid-course corrections to their strategies. The ERT also used the standardized campus data to conduct analyses across the twenty-eight campuses in the project.

---

1 The ERT gathered data disaggregated by race/ethnicity for the University of California and the California State University systems in order to make comparisons on key indicators of undergraduate student access and success as well as faculty hiring. Data from these systems provided some benchmarks for the CDI campuses. However, campus leaders are cautioned about relying on peers as benchmarks when it comes to increasing the presence of URM students or faculty. Peer institutions may not reflect the URM student or faculty pool and thus may cause campuses to set their expectations too low.

It is critical that all data—including survey responses and focus group findings—be disaggregated by race/ethnicity, gender, income level, and other factors that are important to institutional goals for diversity. Disaggregated data frequently yield valuable information about differences in perspectives and experiences among groups. Too often, campus leaders disaggregate only the most basic demographic data on students for inclusion in a viewbook or on a Web site. However, when information about access and success is disaggregated, leaders can learn a great deal more about how all students—and how different groups of students—are faring in their educational experiences.

It is also important that constituents rely on multiple sources of data. Similar findings across different data sets will help constituents speak with some certainty about the status of access, success, and other goals for diversity. Dissimilar findings will point out the need for further examination of a phenomenon. Leaders will find that the most meaningful data will result from incorporating diversity questions into all institutional inquiries and analyses—of student, staff, and faculty satisfaction; of student, staff, and faculty success; of campus climate; and of student learning and engagement. Collecting data at the department, program, and school levels also provides a fuller understanding of the status of faculty, undergraduate and graduate students, and staff in the places on campus where they are most deeply engaged. It is not unusual to discover that some schools or departments are not making progress on one or more diversity dimensions while other units on campus are doing quite well. Such findings can help campus leaders gauge progress at the institutional level, identify promising practices that may translate across campus, and point to places where greater attention to diversity is needed.

Use Multiple Sources of Data to Guide Decision Making

One CDI campus proposed developing a summer bridge program focused on support for URM students in the STEM disciplines as part of its CDI. Campus leaders believed that URM students needed such a program to be competitive and that the program would reduce existing achievement gaps. Yet an analysis of the campus senior survey, GPA, and persistence data across various groups on campus indicated that the decision to start a summer bridge program was not well founded. Disaggregated data revealed that URM students were doing well in their academic pursuits but not adjusting well to campus life because of the small number of URM students at the institution. Campus leaders consequently requested and were approved to have grant funds redirected to a high school outreach program, to help more URM students become college eligible and possibly enroll at the institution. The timely use of campus data helped leaders to avoid establishing a support program that likely would not have improved overall success for URM students.

7. Share Results to Increase Understanding and Commitment across Campus

Data collection, analysis, and reporting processes should be an integral part of campus diversity efforts, but constituents often resist sharing data across the institution. Many constituents may worry that data will cause political fallout if they reveal "bad news." Others may think that data will generate controversy, especially if related to diversity issues. Still others may want to show the institution in the best possible light.

Overcoming this resistance is important and can be done by showing constituents that data analyses will be used for organizational improvement rather than to punish individuals or units. While individuals and units must be held accountable for actions and for outcomes, they should be given the support and resources that will equip them to succeed. It is important to communicate this message to constituents and to back it up with examples of units or departments that have been given the chance to improve their performance on institution-level outcomes.

When constituents from across the institution gather and make sense of the data in the context of their own work, they will foster organizational learning and relationships built around shared goals and responsibilities. Just as the committee would benefit from engaging a broader group of constituents in planning, decision making, data analysis, and interpretation of findings, they would benefit from having such a group talk openly and constructively about the consequences of the findings. At this stage, campus presentations on diversity efforts—goals, strategies, findings, progress, and barriers—can help facilitate this dialogue.

To make an appreciable difference, the committee's findings and reports must be valued by senior leaders, shared with the broader campus community, and acted upon in ways that will improve practice. On some CDI campuses, committee reports were not designed for a variety of campus audiences, limiting their utility as vehicles for organizational learning and marginalizing the work they represented.

Convenient and Easy-to-Use Data Make a Difference

On one CDI campus, staff, faculty, and administrators were able to access charts displaying numerical and graphical data through a secure Web-based system. The databases that generated the charts included demographic information on faculty, students, and staff. Users could make specific queries based on their unit or department, examine disaggregated data in order to focus on underrepresented populations, and make comparisons with peer institutions (e.g., regarding faculty racial/ethnic diversity or graduation rates of URM students). To foster broad engagement with the data, the institutional research office staff also made regular presentations at administrative and departmental meetings and other key meetings. These efforts were successful because of the commitment on the part of the institutional research staff to sharing information in formats and through channels that were convenient and easy to use.

8. Assess and Build Capacity to Do the Work

To meet accreditation requirements and public expectations, campuses must demonstrate that they have the intellectual, human, and financial resources to successfully undertake their research, teaching, and service functions. These resources represent the capacity of an institution to fulfill its mission and effectively operate on a day-to-day basis. Likewise, campuses will require a certain amount of capacity to successfully fulfill broad goals for diversity. Resources may be internal or external to the institution, but campus leaders should be careful not to rely too heavily on time-limited, external resources such as grant funds. These funds should be leveraged to help build internal capacity to do comprehensive diversity work.

> **Make Good Use of Existing Tools and Resources**
>
> Leaders should first look to their own campus to identify individuals who can assist in developing, implementing, and evaluating diversity initiatives. If people with the necessary knowledge cannot be found, leaders should consider using external experts in diversity and evaluation. Campus leaders can also identify diversity-related conferences and institutes to help build expertise among constituents. These events provide opportunities to discuss concerns and difficulties, learn about promising practices, refine goals and strategies, and even obtain individual coaching. Constituents can also increase the impact of these knowledge-building events by sharing information once they are back on campus.

9. Establish an Infrastructure to Sustain Organizational Learning

In undertaking comprehensive diversity work, campus leaders often struggle with whether to begin by developing an "infrastructure" for diversity (e.g., establishing a diversity office, hiring a chief diversity officer, meaningfully embedding a diversity into the mission statement) or by delving into the work itself (e.g., establishing a faculty re-granting program or revising URM student recruitment efforts). On the one hand, campus leaders may decide to invest in an infrastructure, but the seeming delay in creating tangible change can generate significant tension among constituents. On the other hand, leaders may decide to use existing resources to launch the actual work, but that work can falter unless personnel, facilities, policies, and other "scaffolding" are put in place to support it.

The ERT discovered that campuses were most successful when leaders attended to both components simultaneously—that is, when campus leaders invested in an infrastructure while also launching a few visible efforts that were likely to make a difference relatively quickly and without needing all aspects of an infrastructure in place.

In addition to consultations and meetings, there are many material resources campuses can draw on in this work. These include published studies, research journals, and articles on topics such as faculty hiring; relevant Web sites (e.g., www.DiversityWeb.org) and bibliographies on diversity and evaluation; survey instruments;

frameworks for diversity; and data workbooks to guide the collection of campus data. The *CDI Evaluation Project Resource Kit* includes all of the above (see appendix 4 for more information).

Whenever a campus is engaged in major planning or evaluation efforts, constituents should discuss the potential impact of choices and decisions on diversity efforts. This applies to budgeting, "downsizing," strategic planning, fundraising, expanding curricular offerings, and engaging in accreditation processes, to name just a few activities. If a campus has a chief diversity officer, he or she should be actively involved in such discussions to ensure that diversity is "at the table." Just as the chief financial officer ensures that budget implications are discussed in all decision-making processes, so should the chief diversity officer be empowered to raise important questions about diversity and ask leaders to consider the consequences of their actions—good, bad, or neutral—vis-à-vis diversity.

Finally, with each personnel transition on a campus, institutional knowledge and history regarding evaluation or diversity work is diminished. Because transitions are inevitable, campus leaders should develop processes to help diversity work weather transitions. This includes preserving knowledge (keeping a library of electronic and print resources), sharing knowledge (passing along relevant information from external and internal meetings and other sources), and transferring knowledge (providing sufficient time so that information can be transferred to new employees). Having a senior position dedicated to the diversity initiative can also help maintain an evolving knowledge base.

Four Critical Components of Diversity Capacity

1. Sufficient levels of human resources and internal expertise to mount a comprehensive diversity effort
2. Sufficient time for a broad base of campus constituents to plan, implement, and monitor the work
3. Sufficient financial and material resources to support comprehensive efforts, plus a broad awareness of available resources
4. Opportunities and mechanisms to communicate and engage with the campus community about the work

Conclusion

This monograph began with a discussion of the broad changes occurring in higher education over the last half century and how those changes have produced new dilemmas that require new solutions. These dilemmas include
- the persistent achievement gap among racial/ethnic groups and a tendency to focus on "fixing" students through remediation instead of putting in place the institutional structures, policies, and practices that can better ensure educational success for all students;
- the lack of racial/ethnic diversity within the faculty, staff, administrative, and trustee ranks, which seriously inhibits the intellectual power and innovation a diverse constituency can bring to these critical roles and to the education, research, and service functions of the academy;
- the lack of comprehensive systems for evaluation and assessment, particularly those that demonstrate the impact that diversity can have on critical institutional functions, such as curriculum and scholarship;
- the tendency to bypass sustained campus dialogue about the meaning(s) of diversity for a particular institution, as well as a tendency to implement activities that are piecemeal or narrow in scope.

The future of diversity work requires serious reflection on the part of campus leaders. As they seek to strengthen individual institutions and U.S. higher education overall, these leaders should attend to the racial/ethnic diversity of the student body, but also recognize that under a broad diversity framework, compositional diversity can no longer serve as the sole marker of success. Leaders must recognize that for both institutional viability and larger economic, social, and global well-being, diversity work must be conceived of and enacted in comprehensive and intentional ways, where progress on goals can be monitored and adjustments made.

This monograph offers a blueprint for such work, including steps that leaders at all levels can take to achieve campus-wide goals for diversity. The ERT found that effectively addressing the dilemmas described above involved a shift in both mindset and practice—deepening constituents' shared commitment as well as helping them to undertake individual and unit-level efforts that fed into this broad vision. This shift also involved encouraging constituents to approach the work with a sense of innovation and experimentation; helping them translate promising practices into their specific contexts; and creating a culture where data were used for educational improvement and overall organizational effectiveness.

Findings from the Campus Diversity Initiative Evaluation Project suggest that institutional excellence begins with deep connections between diversity work and institutional mission, and that each new milestone is reached through strategic, pragmatic, and principled action. The CDI campuses also demonstrated that leadership for comprehensive diversity work must be developed at all levels and across the institution, and that achieving institutional goals for diversity requires having in place coordinating structures and evaluation processes that will measure progress and enrich individual and organizational learning.

A significant measure of how well diversity efforts were linked to core institutional functioning related to the ways in which diversity was part of the work of all faculty and staff. Some CDI campuses lacked sufficient integration of diversity efforts with "mainstream" issues of institutional planning, effectiveness, accreditation, budget, and overall mission fulfillment. While there was progress in linking diversity to what it means to be a successful institution in California in the twenty-first century, diversity work was too easily moved away from these other issues, to a parallel path where it proceeded without the same level of support.

A diversity initiative had greater potential for success when constituents aligned it with the institution's mission and culture. This alignment was established in part through embedding language about the role of diversity in achieving institutional goals in the campus mission statement as well as in strategic planning and accreditation documents. Having diversity embedded in these key documents was both an indication of the depth and breadth of efforts at a campus as well as part of a strategy for sustaining diversity efforts so that they could become an indisputable part of the culture. When aligned, the institution's mission, culture, and diversity efforts were mutually reinforcing.

The "academic work" of diversity was critical to an initiative's success. Connecting diversity to the scholarly interests of faculty, to the development of the curriculum (in both general education and the majors), and to new approaches to pedagogy were essential for sustaining and deepening diversity as a core part of educational effectiveness and institutional excellence. At the same time, making diversity central to student learning and success—the degree to which different racial/ethnic groups thrived academically and all students developed the competencies to function in a diverse society—complemented faculty work. This intellectual core also served to draw URM students into graduate school and the faculty pipeline, and engaged new URM faculty more deeply on campus.

Another important element for success involved having supportive and engaged leadership at many levels of the institution—including the board of trustees, president, provost, deans, faculty, staff, and students. On the CDI campuses, effective senior leaders played a particularly important role in guiding efforts, contributing to them, and holding campus constituents accountable for making progress. These leaders were most successful when they kept a broad context for the work at the forefront through the use of a diversity framework. The framework enabled leaders at all levels to systematically monitor progress by focusing on a common set of indicators.

The chief diversity officer played a key leadership role, especially when the individual in this role understood the importance of organizational learning in changing institutional culture and practice with respect to diversity. On many of the CDI campuses, this person implemented timely and effective processes (e.g., a regular review of data), coordinated the work of campus constituents, and sought greater involvement from across the institution. Having the chief diversity officer participate in core institutional decision making was one way to provide both continuity and depth in sustaining diversity efforts. At the same time, it was important that the person not be viewed as having to perform all the work of diversity or be solely accountable for all aspects of diversity. When the chief diversity officer coordinated and monitored efforts and involved other constituents in meaningful ways throughout the process, these efforts developed a synergy that carried the larger initiative beyond what could have been accomplished individually.

It was important for CDI campus leaders to meaningfully engage a broad group of constituents in the interpretation of data as well as communicate findings widely across the institution. This helped to increase understanding about what was occurring on campus, broaden involvement with diversity, and create opportunities to expand leadership for action. A number of the campuses also experienced increased involvement with diversity among their boards of trustees, and this helped with sustaining broad-based efforts as well. Maintaining a cadre of leaders throughout the institution who were active in diversity efforts was essential for high-quality decision making and for sustaining progress over time.

Another important element for success involved developing a culture of organizational learning throughout the institution. Organizational learning, like diversity work, interrupts many usual practices and thus is not simple to embed into institutional culture. Because of a tendency to compartmentalize tasks, data collection on CDI campuses—like diversity work—often ended up on a parallel path with "mainstream" campus concerns and had little influence on decision making. Even on CDI campuses where data were being collected and used to inform decisions, the data were often not disaggregated by race/ethnicity, income status, and other factors the campuses themselves deemed important. Few campuses had a broad-based group of constituents who were experienced in effectively managing and disaggregating data. Some were building capacity in this area, recognizing that monitoring disaggregated data was essential to all aspects of comprehensive diversity work and necessary for organizational learning.

Establishing benchmarks was another important element of success. Although not an easy task, benchmarks enabled campus leaders to articulate specific, campus-wide aspirations and provided markers against which leaders could judge the institution's progress. In some cases, however, benchmarks set against peers who were themselves making minimal progress allowed the institutions to make small gains and declare "mission accomplished." This, in turn, prompted the campuses to return to "business as usual," forgoing the organizational learning that would help them to continuously improve efforts.

Fostering a culture of learning also required rich notions of student success. It was troubling—especially in light of recent calls for greater accountability for student learning and achievement in higher education—that most of the CDI campuses ended up focusing narrowly on persistence and graduation rates when monitoring student success across racial/ethnic groups. Such a focus left out other readily available success data that the ERT felt were important to collect and disaggregate.[1] A focus on persistence and graduation rates also revealed nothing about whether students—particularly from underrepresented groups—were achieving key learning outcomes around which there is an emerging, broad-based consensus.[2]

As part of the diversity framework, all CDI campuses were provided a set of indicators that would have revealed much more about whether students across racial/ethnic and income groups were succeeding at equitable levels. Some CDI campuses that were also participating in the Diversity Scorecard Project did collect such data, and a few of these institutions made substantial progress in both raising faculty awareness about the disparities among groups of students and developing action plans to address the inequities.[3] Campuses that focused on high achievement goals for all students while being particularly attentive to underrepresented groups also made gains on the indicators for which data were available.

While persistence and graduation were important elements of success, focusing on those alone risked signaling that "survival-to-degree" was the ultimate goal of a college education rather than preparing students intellectually, cognitively, socially, and emotionally for leadership in the twenty-first century. Having this "survivor" focus in the context of increasing the success of underrepresented students also risked maintaining educational disparities across racial/ethnic groups. CDI campuses achieved greater progress when leaders communicated to constituents the need to hold greater expectations for *all* students and when they supported actions—in the curriculum, in pedagogy, in learning opportunities outside the classroom—that aligned with these high expectations.

A final element of success related to counteracting the personal cost that the previously mentioned dilemmas can exert upon individuals in our institutions. When diversity work is marginalized, whether because of resistance or because of a structure of "silos" on our campuses, longtime champions often bear the brunt of the fallout and disappointment resulting from failure or limited success. Indeed, burnout was a sub-

---

1 These include participation in honors programs; transfer out of majors, particularly the STEM disciplines; participation in study abroad programs; success in "gateway" courses and limited enrollment or "high-demand" programs (e.g., premedical, pre-law, engineering, business); and access to graduate programs.

2 These outcomes include knowledge of human cultures and the natural and physical world, intellectual and practical skills, individual and social responsibility, and integrative learning (AAC&U 2007).

3 The Diversity Scorecard Project, funded by the James Irvine Foundation, was designed to improve institutional effectiveness with the goal of closing achievement gaps among groups of students. The project later became the Equity Scorecard Project. For more information, see www.usc.edu/dept/education/CUE/projects/index.htm.

stantial problem on the CDI campuses throughout the project, and this was especially true at institutions where it was not clear that the efforts of dedicated people were making a real difference at the institutional level.

Given this reality, it is all the more important that campuses avoid generating excitement with pronouncements about diversity only to have this excitement dashed by isolation, lack of support, and lack of progress. The talk of diversity must move beyond lip-service to shared commitment demonstrated through intentional action. As Senator Barbara Mikulski noted, speaking about political leadership, "If you only talk, and don't produce, you are just one more disappointment. You contribute to the cynicism" (Mikulski et al. 2000, 32).

It is the goal of this monograph to provide campus leaders with concrete strategies to help individuals across campus undertake efforts that will make an appreciable difference in achieving campus-wide goals for diversity. Campuses must increase their capacity to harness the creativity and strengths of *all* of their constituents—students, faculty, administrators, staff, and trustees—to enrich all parts of the institution's functioning through comprehensive diversity work. This is critical not only for the academy's continuing educational, academic, and societal legitimacy, but also for the well-being of our students, our nation, and our global community.

References

Association of American Colleges and Universities. 2007. *College learning for the new global century.* Washington, DC: Association of American Colleges and Universities.

Association of American Colleges and Universities. 2002. *Greater expectations: A new vision for learning as a nation goes to college.* Washington, DC: Association of American Colleges and Universities.

Astin, H. S., A. L. Antonio, C. M. Cress, and A. W. Astin. 1997. *Race and ethnicity in the American professoriate, 1995–1996.* Los Angeles: Higher Education Research Institute.

Bauman, G. L., L. T. Bustillos, E. M. Bensimon, M. C. Brown, and R. D. Bartee. 2005. *Achieving equitable educational outcomes with all students: The institution's roles and responsibilities.* Washington, DC: Association of American Colleges and Universities. www.aacu.org/inclusive_excellence/documents/Bauman_et_al.pdf.

Bial, D. 2004. Alternative measures for college admissions: A relational study of a new predictor for success. PhD diss., Harvard University.

Borrego, S. 2003. *Class matters: Beyond access to inclusion.* Washington, DC: NASPA: Student Affairs Administrators in Higher Education.

Bransford, J. D., A. L. Brown, and R. R. Cocking, eds. 1999. *How people learn: Brain, mind, experience, and school.* Washington, DC: National Academy Press.

Campbell, M., and C. McClintock. 2002. Shall we dance? Program evaluation meets OD in the nonprofit sector. *OD Practitioner* 34 (4): 3–7.

Center for Higher Education Policy Analysis. 2004. *The road ahead: Improving diversity in graduate education.* Los Angeles: Center for Higher Education Policy Analysis. www.usc.edu/dept/chepa/pdf/ImprovingDiversity.pdf.

Comer, J. P. 2004. *Leave no child behind: Preparing today's youth for tomorrow's world.* New Haven, CT: Yale University Press.

Crenshaw, K., N. T. Gotanda, G. Peller, and K. Thomas, eds. 1996. *Critical race theory: The key writings that formed the movement.* New York: New Press.

Cross, K. P. 2002. *Learning intensive universities for the twenty-first century.* Prepared for the conference on Mission, Values and Identity, July 13, 2002, Illinois State University, Normal, IL.

Curry, B. K. 1992. *Instituting enduring innovations: Achieving continuity of change in higher education.* ASHE-ERIC Higher Education Report No. 7. Washington, DC: The George Washington University, School of Education and Human Development.

Donovan, M. S., J. D. Bransford, and J. W. Pellegrino, eds. 1999. *How people learn: Bridging research and practice.* Washington, DC: National Academy Press.

Dowd, A. C. 2005. *Data don't drive: Building a practitioner-driven culture of inquiry to assess community college performance.* Indianapolis, IN: Lumina Foundation.

Eckel, P., M. Green, and B. Hill. 2001. *Riding the waves of change: Insights from transforming institutions.* Washington, DC: American Council on Education.

Ewell, P. 2004. *General education and the assessment reform agenda.* Washington, DC: Association of American Colleges and Universities.

Ferguson, M. 2005. *Advancing liberal education: Assessment practices on campus.* Washington, DC: Association of American Colleges and Universities.

Gándara, P., C. Horn, and G. Orfield. 2005. The access crisis in higher education. *Educational Policy* 19 (2): 255–61.

Gay, G. 2000. *Culturally responsive teaching: Theory, research and practice.* New York: Teachers College Press.

Gay, G. 1994. *At the essence of learning: Multicultural education.* West Lafayette, IN: Kappa Delta Pi.

Guinier, L., and G. Torres. 2002. *The miner's canary: Enlisting race, resisting power, transforming democracy.* Cambridge, MA: Harvard University Press.

Gurin, P. 1999. Expert report of Patricia Gurin. In *Gratz, et al. v. Bollinger, et al.* No. 97-75321 (E.D. Mich.) and *Grutter,* No. 97-75928 (E.D. Mich.). www.vpcomm.umich.edu/admissions/legal/expert/gurintoc.html.

Gurin P., J. S. Lehman, and E. L. Lewis. 2004. *Defending diversity: Affirmative action at the University of Michigan.* Ann Arbor, MI: University of Michigan Press.

Harper, S. 2006. *Black male students at public flagship universities in the U.S.: Status, trends, and implications for policy and practice.* Washington, DC: Joint Center for Political and Economic Studies.

Hernandez, G., and M. G. Visher. 2001. *Creating a culture of inquiry.* San Francisco: The James Irvine Foundation.

Hersh, R. H. 2005. What does college teach? It's time to put an end to "faith-based" acceptance of higher education's quality. *The Atlantic Monthly* 296 (4): 140.

Hill-Collins, P. 2000. *Black feminist thought: Knowledge, consciousness, and the politics of empowerment.* Revised 10th anniversary edition. New York: Routledge.

Hrabowski, F. A. III. 2004. Leadership for a new age: Higher education's role in producing minority leaders. *Liberal Education* 90 (2): 26–33. www.aacu.org/liberaleducation/le-sp04/le-sp04feature2.cfm.

Hurtado, S., J. F. Milem, A. R. Clayton-Pedersen, and W. R. Allen. 1999. *Enacting diverse learning environments: Improving the climate for racial/ethnic diversity in higher education.* ASHE-ERIC Higher Education Reports Series 26 (8). San Francisco: Jossey-Bass.

Ibarra, R. A. 2001. *Beyond affirmative action: Reframing the context of higher education.* Madison, WI: The University of Wisconsin Press.

Jaschik, S. 2006. Michigan votes down affirmative action. *Inside Higher Education* (November 8), www.insidehighered.com/news/2006/11/08/michigan.

Kim, W. 2006. Supreme Court takes aim at affirmative action. *DiversityInc.com* (June 6), www.diversityinc.com/public/21571.cfm (subscription required).

Kuh, G. D., J. Kinzie, J. H. Schuh, E. J. Whitt and Associates. 2005. *Student success in college: Creating conditions that matter.* San Francisco: Jossey-Bass.

Lee, S. J. 1996. *Unraveling the "model minority" stereotype: Listening to Asian American youth.* New York: Teachers College Press.

Leskes, A., and R. Miller. 2006. *Purposeful pathways: Helping students achieve key learning outcomes.* Washington, DC: Association of American Colleges and Universities.

Lopez, A. 2002. *The largest American Indian populations in California: Household and family data from the Census 2000.* Race and Ethnicity in California: Demographics Report Series No. 7. Stanford, CA: Center for Comparative Studies in Race and Ethnicity. ccsre.stanford.edu/reports/report_7.pdf.

Maruyama, G., and J. F. Moreno. 2000. University faculty views about the value of diversity on campus and in the classroom. In *Does diversity make a difference? Three research studies on diversity in college classrooms*, 9–35. Washington, DC: American Council on Education and American Association of University Professors.

Meacham, J., and C. Barrett. 2003. Commitment to diversity in institutional mission statements. *Diversity Digest* 7 (1/2): 6–7, 9.

Mikulski, B., K. B. Hutchison, D. Feinstein, B. Boxer, P. Murray, O. Snowe, S. Collins, M. Landrieu, and B. L. Lincoln, with C. Whitney. 2000. *Nine and counting: The women of the Senate.* New York: William Morrow and Company.

Milem, J. F. 1999. *The importance of faculty diversity to student learning and to the mission of higher education.* Paper presented at the American Council on Education symposium and working meeting on diversity and affirmative action. Washington, DC: American Council on Education.

Milem, J. F., M. Chang, and A. Antonio. 2005. *Making diversity work on campus: A research-based perspective.* Washington, DC: Association of American Colleges and Universities.

Milem, J. F., E. L. Dey, and C. B. White. 2004. Diversity considerations in health professions education. In *In the nation's compelling interest: Ensuring diversity in the health care workforce*, ed. B. D. Smedley, A. S. Butler, and L. R. Bristow, 345–90. Washington, DC: The National Academies Press.

Miller, R., and A. Leskes. 2005. *Levels of assessment: From the student to the institution.* Washington, DC: Association of American Colleges and Universities.

Moreno, J. F., D. G. Smith, A. R. Clayton-Pedersen, S. Parker, and D. H. Teraguchi. 2006a. *The revolving door for underrepresented minority faculty in higher education.* San Francisco: The James Irvine Foundation. www.irvine.org/assets/pdf/pubs/education/insight_Revolving_Door.pdf.

Moreno, J. F., D. G. Smith, S. Parker, A. R. Clayton-Pedersen, and D. H. Teraguchi. 2006b. *Using multiple lenses: An examination of the economic and racial/ethnic diversity of college students.* San Francisco: The James Irvine Foundation. www.irvine.org/assets/pdf/pubs/education/insight_Multiple_Lenses.pdf.

Musil, C. M., M. García, C. A. Hudgins, M. T. Nettles, W. E. Sedlacek, and D. G. Smith. 1999. *To form a more perfect union: Campus diversity initiatives.* Washington, DC: Association of American Colleges and Universities.

Orfield, G., and D. Whitla. 2001. *Diversity challenged: Evidence of the impact of affirmative action.* Boston: Harvard Education Publishing Group.

Pew Charitable Trusts, Planning and Evaluation Department. 2001. *Returning results: Planning and evaluation at the Pew Charitable Trusts.* Philadelphia: Pew Charitable Trusts.

Preskill, H., and R. T. Torres. 1999. *Evaluative inquiry for learning in organizations.* Thousand Oaks, CA: Sage Publications.

Schmidt, P. 2006. From "minority" to "diversity." *The Chronicle of Higher Education* 52 (22): A24.

Sedlacek, W. E. 2004. *Beyond the big test: Noncognitive assessment in higher education.* San Francisco: Jossey-Bass.

Senge, P. 2006. *The fifth discipline: The art and practice of the learning organization.* Rev. ed. New York: Doubleday.

Shafritz, J. M., J. S. Ott, and Y. S. Jang. 2005. *Classics of organization theory.* 6th ed. Belmont, CA: Thomson Wadsworth.

Shulman, L. S. 2005. Excellence: An immodest proposal. Palo Alto, CA: The Carnegie Foundation for the Advancement of Teaching. www.carnegiefoundation.org/perspectives/sub.asp?key=245&subkey=1252.

Smith, D. G. 1995. Organizational implications of diversity in higher education. In *Diversity in organizations,* ed. M. Chemers, S. Oskamp, and M. Costanzo, 220–44. Newbury Park, CA: Sage Publications.

Smith, D. G. 1997. The progress of a decade: An imperative for the future. Unpublished report on The James Irvine Foundation's Higher Education Diversity Initiative.

Smith, D. G., J. F. Moreno, A. R. Clayton-Pedersen, S. Parker, and D. H. Teraguchi. 2005. *"Unknown" students on college campuses: An exploratory analysis.* San Francisco: The James Irvine Foundation. www.irvine.org/assets/pdf/pubs/education/UnknownStudentsCDI.pdf.

Smith, D. G., S. Parker, A. R. Clayton-Pedersen, J. F. Moreno, and D. H. Teraguchi. 2006. *Building capacity: A study of the impact of the James Irvine Foundation Campus Diversity Initiative.* San Francisco: The James Irvine Foundation. www.irvine.org/assets/pdf/pubs/education/cdi_Eval_Impact_Study.pdf.

Steele, C. 2003. Stereotype threat and African-American student achievement. In *Young, gifted, and black: Promoting high achievement among African-American students,* ed. T. Perry, C. Steele and A. Hilliard III, 109–30. Boston: Beacon Press.

Takaki, R. 1989. *Strangers from a different shore: A history of Asian Americans.* Boston: Little, Brown, and Company.

Williams, D. A., J. B. Berger, and S. A. McClendon. 2005. *Toward a model of inclusive excellence and change in postsecondary institutions.* Washington, DC: Association of American Colleges and Universities. www.aacu.org/inclusive_excellence/documents/Williams_et_al.pdf.

Williams, D. A., and K. C. Wade-Golden. 2006. What is a chief diversity officer? *Inside Higher Ed* (April 18). www.insidehighered.com/workplace/2006/04/18/williams.

W. K. Kellogg Foundation. 1998. *W. K. Kellogg Foundation evaluation handbook.* Battle Creek, MI: Kellogg.

Wu, F. H. 2003. *Yellow: Race in America beyond black and white*. New York: Basic Books.

Appendix 1
Campus strategies by dimension*

STRATEGIES BY DIMENSION OF DIVERSITY	n	% (n/28)**
ACCESS AND SUCCESS		
Access		
Admissions-Undergraduate		
Outreach/Pre-College	15	54%
Admissions	6	21%
Financial Aid	4	14%
Admissions-Graduate		
Fellowships	5	18%
Admissions/Outreach	1	4%
Subtotal	22***	79%
Success		
Undergraduate		
Student Support Services	16	57%
Mentoring/Peer Advising	8	29%
Student Involvement with Faculty Research	5	18%
Summer Academic Support Programs	1	4%
Graduate		
Program/Development	3	11%
Subtotal	18***	64%
CAMPUS CLIMATE/INTERGROUP RELATIONS		
Student Campus Programming	15	54%
Multicultural Center	1	4%
Subtotal	16***	57%
EDUCATION AND SCHOLARSHIP		
Faculty Workshops/Seminars	17	61%
Pedagogy/Curriculum Change	16	57%
Faculty Prepartion/Professional Development	14	50%
Faculty Research	7	25%
Study Abroad	2	7%
Subtotal	19***	68%
INSTITUTIONAL VIABILITY AND VITALITY		
Assessment/Evaluation/IR	22	79%
Faculty Hiring	16	57%
Diversity-related Support Staff	15	54%
Campus-based Diversity Education	12	43%
Community Outreach	11	39%
CDO/Senior Diversity Person	6	21%
Postdocs	4	14%
Administrative Hiring	3	11%
Subtotal	28***	100%

*Strategies for access and success are divided out to provide greater detail to the reader. **% campuses employing a particular strategy or employing strategies within a particular category. ***Total number of campuses employing *any* strategy in the previous category (some campuses employed more than one strategy within a category).

Appendix 2
CDI Evaluation Project Institutionalization Rubric

Overview

A key goal of the Campus Diversity Initiative was to facilitate change with respect to diversity in ways that would foster the success of underrepresented minority and low-income students and build institutional capacity to function more successfully with respect to diversity. An important part of the CDI Evaluation Project was to assist campuses in deepening and broadening their evaluation efforts so that their diversity work could be sustained over time. The project sought to assess institutional change by answering the question: "Overall, have institutions changed in terms of depth, breadth, and institutionalization of diversity?" (Smith et al. 2006).

Developing a generic instrument to evaluate the degree of institutional change was difficult because of the differences among the institutions involved in the project and the challenge of making judgments that took these differences into account. Nevertheless, the literature on organizational change, especially as relates to higher education, does offer analytical frameworks to evaluate the degree of change.

For example, in a monograph produced by the American Council on Education, the authors proposed using a depth and breadth analysis to capture the level of change on a particular campus (Eckel, Green, and Hill 2001). In addition, an earlier review of the James Irvine Foundation's diversity efforts (Smith 1997) and the results of a national evaluation study of diversity (Musil et al. 1999) suggest that depth, breadth, and institutionalization can be ascertained through a number of indicators. When specific changes become a permanent part of an organization's functions, those changes can be considered to be institutionalized. Institutionalization is critical to the topics addressed in this monograph, for it is widely known that "when a change is not institutionalized, it is likely to be terminated" (Curry 1992, iii).

The ERT synthesized all of the quantitative and qualitative data collected through the CDI Evaluation Project to analyze the degree of institutionalization of diversity efforts at the individual campuses and across the twenty-eight campuses. As part of this process, the ERT developed a rubric to examine differences in the degree of institutionalization from the beginning to the end of the CDI.

The institutionalization rubric consists of five elements—goals, resources, capacity, leadership, and centrality—each with a scale of 0–10. The ERT designed the scales to capture changes in institutional conditions and individual behaviors and demonstrate levels of depth and breadth in five areas critical to the success of comprehensive diversity work. Raters gave a campus a score on each element to reflect the extent to which the five elements were present and the extent to which a campus made progress on them over time. At least two people from the ERT assigned rubric scores to a subset of the campuses to assess reliability. The overall reliability of the rubric scores was 70 percent, suggesting reasonable inter-rater reliability.

> **Five elements necessary for the success of comprehensive diversity work**
>
> 1. Goals—diversity is widely accepted and known as an institutional goal
> 2. Resources—resources (e.g., human, financial, space) exist to mount efforts
> 3. Capacity—capacity exists to undertake and sustain efforts
> 4. Leadership—leadership development for diversity is both broad and deep and leaders at all levels are organized through some institution-wide mechanism
> 5. Centrality—efforts are connected to core institutional functions

There is overlap among the elements, and they are somewhat sequential. For example, building a high level of institutional capacity requires that individuals have a high level of understanding and acceptance of institutional goals as well as the resources necessary to be successful. When several of the elements were present at high levels, they tend to be mutually reinforcing.

Rubric Instructions

The five elements that comprise the rubric are most directly linked to the institutional viability and vitality dimension of Smith's (1995) diversity framework. Campus leaders can use the rubric when they are embarking upon comprehensive diversity work or when they are beginning to make current efforts more comprehensive by connecting, strengthening, or monitoring existing work. The initial scoring establishes a baseline against which subsequent ratings can be compared and analyzed to ascertain the degree of change. Based on experiences within the CDI, the ERT recommends that campus leaders use the rubric annually to monitor overall progress in institutionalizing diversity. It is useful for leaders to keep in mind the five elements and previous scores as they learn about specific diversity-related activities taking place and work with campus constituents to meet institution-wide goals for diversity.

The one-page score sheets that follow describe the general optimal conditions for each element. A rater would assign an institution a score based on specific campus conditions and actions that reflect a particular level of depth, breadth, and institutionalization. When assigning a score, the rater should take into account all available campus data, including official documents, survey results, observations, and interviews. The rater should then list the types and sources of data he or she is using to determine the score in the comments section of each sheet.

When it is time to make comparisons of progress against previous rubric scores, campus leaders can refer to the information in the comments sections in order to connect specific actions and events to changes in scores, to create a rich story of campus action, and to describe the collective influence that comprehensive diversity work is having across the campus.

It is important to remember that a rubric is only *valuable* when it informs and enhances the work it intends to measure. Use of the rubric will require personnel and time, and so it should be used in a context where it can truly influence activity. Campus leaders should analyze both the quantitative ratings and the qualitative reporting to determine the rubric's reliability and value in charting institutional progress on diversity.

Note: Since the rubric was designed to capture external reviewers' perceptions of institutionalization of comprehensive diversity work across multiple campuses, the authors are very interested in learning about the usefulness of the rubric as a self-assessment tool for individual campuses. Feedback about its use can be forwarded to cdimonograph@aacu.org.

CDI Evaluation Project Institutionalization Rubric Score Sheet:
Goals

General Conditions—the extent to which constituents know about and understand institutional goals for diversity and the comprehensive diversity work needed to achieve the goals. The presence of this element is indicated by the following conditions:

- The goals are articulated in institutional statements that guide the work of various units (e.g., mission statements, strategic planning documents, human resources policies) as well as in campus periodic documents (e.g., newspaper editorials, alumni newsletters).
- Campus leaders have articulated in writing how institutional goals for diversity and related comprehensive work connect to various institutional functions.
- The institutional goals for diversity and the comprehensive work needed to achieve them are clearly communicated to constituents vis-à-vis their roles and responsibilities (e.g., in job descriptions, performance review documents).
- Constituents can articulate their own and their units' specific roles and responsibilities in achieving institutional goals for diversity. Constituents also understand the roles and responsibilities of constituents with whom they must collaborate to achieve the goals.
- Individuals, units, and the campus as a whole can demonstrate that efforts are helping to make progress on institutional goals for diversity.

Scoring Key

0   None of the general conditions are present.

1–2   Goals may appear sporadically in one or two periodic documents but not in any institutional statements; the goals are understood and acted on by a very small number of people within a single unit or by a very small number of individuals across the institution; the people involved can only partially articulate their own roles and responsibilities in achieving the goals and have limited or no understanding of the roles and responsibilities of others. Efforts are based on conventional wisdom, and progress is not monitored.

3–4   Goals appear in some periodic documents and institutional statements. Much of work undertaken to achieve goals is limited to one whole unit or parts of a small number of units across the campus. Those involved may not be completely clear about the purpose of the action, the intended outcomes, or their particular roles and responsibilities. Some aspects of the work is based on research and data about what works. Monitoring of progress is limited (e.g., gathering perceptions about the actions from those doing the work).

5–6   Goals are regularly articulated in periodic documents and in many institutional statements. The work needed to achieve institutional goals for diversity is undertaken across a number of institutional roles and units, and individuals doing the work are clear on the purpose of the action and the outcomes. Much of the work is based on research and data about what works. Progress is more regularly monitored but only in basic ways.

7–8   Goals are regularly articulated in all periodic documents and in institutional statements. The work needed to achieve institutional goals for diversity is enacted across most institutional roles and units, and there is a broad base of people who understand the purpose of the action, can articulate their own and others' roles in ensuring the intended outcomes, and take responsibility for achieving the goals. Efforts are steeped in research and data about what works, and campus-based data alerts constituents as to whether practices are successful locally. Progress toward goals is consistently monitored in sophisticated ways by a broad base of constituents, and results are broadly shared.

9–10   All of the conditions listed in the 7–8 score are present, plus those groups and activities affected by actions are sources of evidence that the actions made an appreciable difference. Depending on the goals for a particular campus, curriculum will be revised, student learning outcomes related to diversity (e.g., cognitive complexity, intercultural competence) will be enhanced, access and success of underrepresented students will be increased, campus climate will be improved, and conventional notions of scholarship will be expanded. Evidence of progress should move beyond measuring simple "exposure" to diversity to assessing meaningful engagement that imparts learning, contributes to disciplines, or tangibly contributes to institutional mission and vitality.

Score: _____

Rater's Name: _____

Comments (Raters should provide supporting materials that justify the score assigned in this area, such as institutional documents, meeting notes, and summaries of conversations with various campus constituent groups.)

CDI Evaluation Project Institutionalization Rubric Score Sheet:
Resources

General Conditions—the extent to which the resources necessary to achieve institutional goals for diversity are made available and are known to constituents across the institution. The extent to which individuals undertaking comprehensive diversity work are capable of using the resources to achieve the goals. The presence of this element is indicated by the following conditions:

- Personnel (people), space, time, and financial resources are allocated to the initiative.
- Allocations are discussed among individuals within and across the involved units and discussed in light of each unit's and the institution's resource demands.
- During budget allocation processes, campus leaders discuss institutional goals for diversity and the resources necessary for achieving them. Allocations are sufficient to carry out comprehensive action.
- Actions to achieve institutional goals for diversity are sustained by the institution, independent of external resources.
- Resource allocations are monitored and adjusted based on data regarding need.

Scoring Key

0   None of the general conditions are present.

1–2   Some personnel time is allocated to diversity work but this time is limited to a very small number of people or to a single unit. Some space, time, and financial resources are available for short-term programs and projects or specific ad hoc tasks. A single unit is responsible for diversity work, but there is little collaborative effort among the people in the responsible unit. Monitoring progress is limited to recognizing that resource deficiencies exist and that accomplishing institutional goals will be difficult.

3–4   A small number of people within one or two units are designated to undertake diversity work. Resources within or across these units may be insufficiently linked to carry out tasks needed to achieve institutional goals for diversity. Time, space, and financial resources are made available for longer-term projects and programs, but the amounts are inadequate to make substantial progress toward goals. Resource allocation decisions are made solely in response to crises or conventional wisdom rather than based on data showing need.

5–6   Many people within a unit—or several people within a small number of units—are responsible for achieving institutional goals for diversity. People across these units take responsibility for diversity work and there is some synergy with regard to resource use within and across these units. Space, time, and financial resources are approaching adequate levels for making progress toward goals. Resource allocation for diversity work is beginning to be included in strategic planning. Methods and systems to monitor effective resource use and need are being developed.

7–8   Many units and people within them are broadly involved in diversity work. The people and units involved have sufficient time, space, and financial resources to undertake most tasks. Resource allocation is broadly discussed and there is considerable synergy with regard to resource use across units. Current levels of resources enable individuals undertaking diversity work to make substantial progress toward goals. Resource allocation decisions are established as part of strategic planning and are based on data about effective use and need. Methods and systems to monitor effective resource use and need are in place and beginning to be used.

9–10   All of the conditions listed in the 7–8 score are present, plus the institution has aligned resources to achieve institutional goals for diversity in an effective and efficient manner. Resource allocation is regularly based on data about progress toward goals. This score should also reflect an institutional context in which many people at different organizational levels understand the goals, view the work as a viable strategy to achieve the goals, are capable of allocating resources at the levels and in the combination needed across units, and are willing to do so.

Score: _____

Rater's Name: _____

Comments (Raters should provide supporting materials that justify the score assigned in this area, such as institutional documents, meeting notes, and summaries of conversations with various campus constituent groups.)

CDI Evaluation Project Institutionalization Rubric Score Sheet:
Capacity

General Conditions—the extent to which people—individually and collectively—are capable of planning, implementing, monitoring, and sustaining comprehensive diversity work. The extent to which institutional systems and processes are in place to facilitate comprehensive diversity work. The presence of this element is indicated by the following conditions:

- Education and professional development is provided to help campus constituents understand the institutional goals for diversity, as well as the complexity of diversity issues. Constituents also understand how the initiative's components fit together to achieve the goals as well as the nature of change and resistance to it.
- Principled collaborative leadership is practiced that affirms, guides, and coordinates the work of the initiative.
- Leaders establish information, data collection, and communication systems that are integrated, effective, and consistent across the institution. Initiative components are intentionally linked. Data are systematically collected, shared, and used for decision making. Relevant knowledge and information is shared across particular units and across the institution.

Scoring Key

0   None of the general conditions are present.

1–2   Education and professional development is available to a very limited number of people and knowledge gained is not shared beyond the individuals in attendance. Leaders provide very little guidance within units or coordination across units. Systems and processes used to coordinate tasks within and across units are too basic to address the complexity of the work to be accomplished. Monitoring of progress in capacity-building is limited to self reports of learning from the education and professional development that is offered.

3–4   A small number of units offer meaningful education and professional development to individuals who work within those units. Learning is shared among colleagues within the units. Some leaders begin to emphasize communication and collaboration across units, and some individuals begin these activities. Support of institutional goals for diversity is apparent among a select group of leaders, but the support is largely due to individual interest and is not consistently demonstrated over time. Constituents are developing communication channels across units, and leaders are beginning to establish systems to collect and use data and communicate information across the institution.

5–6   Many individuals and units are provided appropriate and effective education and professional development, and learning is broadly shared within and across some units. Some leaders clearly link diversity work to the roles and responsibilities of constituent groups. Broad support of the leadership is apparent, but this support is not yet consistently demonstrated over time. Mechanisms are in place to monitor the effect of education and professional development across constituent groups. Leaders have established systems to collect and use data and communicate information across the institution, and they have developed processes for coordinating efforts across units.

7–8   Many individuals and units are provided highly effective education and professional development. Constituents across units regularly discuss diversity work and review progress toward goals in order to improve efforts. Systems to collect and use data, communicate information across the institution, and coordinate efforts are well developed. Leaders champion the work and consistently link it to the institution's core educational mission. Leaders have substantive data to demonstrate progress. Some leaders are willing to engage constituents in dialogue about missteps revealed through the data.

9–10   All of the conditions listed in the 7–8 score are present, plus sufficient capacity exists across the institution to carry out the work of the initiative. Both leaders and constituents champion the goals and the initiative in ways that consistently link it to the institution's core educational mission. Progress toward goals is consistently monitored. Leaders regularly engage in dialogue about data that demonstrates missteps as well as progress. These data are shared, explored and used to make the case for additional capacity-building.

Score: _____

Rater's Name: _____

Comments (Raters should provide supporting materials that justify the score assigned in this area, such as institutional documents, meeting notes, and summaries of conversations with various campus constituent groups.)

CDI Evaluation Project Institutionalization Rubric Score Sheet:
Leadership

General Conditions—the extent to which leaders at all levels can ensure that institutional goals for diversity are achieved via a successful comprehensive diversity initiative. The presence of this element is indicated by the following conditions:

- Leaders work to ensure that institutional goals for diversity are clearly articulated to constituents at all levels and across campus. Leaders work to ensure that constituents are capable of achieving goals (i.e., possess sufficient knowledge, ability, skills, and resources) and are held accountable for achieving goals.
- Leaders commit or expand internal (i.e., institutional) resources to the initiative in order to rely less on external resources. At the same time, leaders also work to secure external resources to more rapidly scale up efforts or continue progress when internal resources are restricted.
- Current active leaders work to broaden the number of existing leaders who are engaged in the initiative. These leaders also work to expand the group by encouraging and motivating constituents to take on leadership roles related to the initiative.
- Leaders help constituents understand and communicate the initiative's connection to the institution's core educational mission.
- Leaders work to build institutional capacity to succeed, including developing systems to monitor progress toward goals.

Scoring Key

0   None of the general conditions are present.

1–2   A very small number of leaders know and understand the institutional goals for diversity, and this group is held solely responsible for achieving the goals. Most leaders are unwilling to commit their units' internal funds or other resources to the work, and resources mainly come from external sources. Leadership is limited to the unit where the diversity work is anchored, such as multicultural affairs, and leadership development is limited to one or two people in the anchor unit. Little is done to motivate a broad group of leaders and constituents to undertake diversity work. Leaders rarely help constituents link these efforts to the institution's core educational mission. Progress on goals is not monitored.

3–4   Leadership for diversity work exists in a small number of units that have "obvious" connections to the goals. Few leaders beyond these units understand the goals and the work needed to achieve them. A few leaders allocate a small amount of internal resources to foster collaboration across units. Leadership development is limited to individuals in involved units. Some leaders begin to encourage and motivate their constituents to understand the goals, undertake the work, and share responsibility for making progress. Leaders begin to establish basic systems to monitor progress toward goals.

5–6   Leadership is present in a moderate number of units beyond those obviously related to the work. Leaders in these units work to ensure that constituents understand institutional goals for diversity and work to achieve them. Leaders allocate resources to coordinate activities across units. Leadership development opportunities are offered to many constituents in these units. Leaders consistently work to help constituents understand the link between diversity work and institutional mission and values. A number of constituents are held accountable for outcomes of the work. Leaders have ensured that basic systems to monitor progress are in place.

7–8   Leadership is demonstrated at many levels within a unit and in many units across the institution. Institutional goals for diversity are clearly a part of leadership roles and responsibilities. Leaders frequently make decisions that provide adequate resources to undertake diversity work and actively encourage constituents to participate in leadership development activities. Leaders work to establish more sophisticated systems to collect data, and they use the results to inform decision making. Most people and units involved in diversity work are held accountable for the outcomes. Leaders have begun to establish sophisticated systems for monitoring progress.

9–10   All of the conditions listed in the 7–8 score are present, plus leadership for diversity work is evident across most units of the institution, at all leadership levels, and among many constituent groups. Leaders consistently integrate institutional goals for diversity and the work undertaken to achieve them into their planning, decision making, and actions. Leaders work to intentionally align resources to achieve goals, and they consistently motivate others to take on leadership roles within the efforts. Strong advocacy has led to the establishment of sophisticated systems to monitor progress.

Score: _____

Rater's Name: _____

Comments (Raters should provide supporting materials that justify the score assigned in this area, such as institutional documents, meeting notes, and summaries of conversations with various campus constituent groups.)

CDI Evaluation Project Institutionalization Rubric Score Sheet:
Centrality

General Conditions—the extent to which the values espoused by the initiative are central to the institution's mission and day-to-day practices. The presence of these elements is indicated by the following conditions:

- The institution's mission is reflected in the institutional goals for diversity and is embedded in the work undertaken to achieve goals. Likewise, the values represented in these goals and related efforts are reflected in the mission and institutional statements (e.g., strategic plans, progress reports, policies).

- Institutional goals for diversity and the comprehensive diversity initiative are consistently articulated in speeches by leaders and in meetings of governance bodies (e.g., faculty senate, board of trustees).

- The goals and the initiative are consistently taken into consideration in planning and decision making and are reflected in the day-to-day work of constituents at all levels of the institution (e.g., in programs, hiring, community interaction).

Scoring Key

0   None of the general conditions are present.

1–2   Institutional goals for diversity are merely referenced in periodic documents, and diversity work is not connected to institutional mission. Work is comprised of isolated programs and events within a small number of units. Leaders rarely incorporate the goals and the work into their planning, decision making, and actions.

3–4   The smaller numbers of units for doing diversity work acknowledge the institutional goals for diversity in planning and decision making. The goals are articulated in a small number of institutional statements and reports. Isolated work takes place across the unit or units most obviously connected to the diversity goals. Leaders sometimes incorporate the goals and the work into their planning, decision making, and actions.

5–6   Additional units discuss institutional goals for diversity and include them in their planning and decision making. Goals are woven into a number of these units' documents and reports. Work takes place consistently across the units most obviously connected to the diversity goals. Leaders frequently incorporate the goals and the work into their planning, decision making, and actions.

7–8   Many units across campus discuss institutional goals for diversity and include them into their planning and decision making. The goals are articulated in a large number of institutional statements and unit documents and reports. Diversity work takes place across a significant number of units. Leaders consistently incorporate the goals and the work into their planning, decision making, and actions.

9–10 All of the conditions listed in the 7–8 score are present, plus nearly all units include institutional goals for diversity in planning and decision making. The goals are articulated in nearly all institutional statements and unit documents and reports. Comprehensive diversity work is an integral part of the institution's strategic plan and day-to-day functions. The values represented in these goals and related efforts are inextricably linked to institutional mission. Leaders and constituents across campus and at all levels are held accountable for outcomes of diversity work and for making progress toward goals.

Score: _____

Rater's Name: _____

Comments (Raters should provide supporting materials that justify the score assigned in this area, such as institutional documents, meeting notes, and summaries of conversations with various campus constituent groups.)

Appendix 3
Summary of *Guidelines for Creating an Evaluation Plan*

Full document available at: www.aacu.org/irvinediveval/pdfs/Campus_Guidelines.pdf.

Members of the ERT developed these guidelines to help the Campus Diversity Initiative institutions formulate their evaluation plans. The evaluation plans were designed to help leaders (a) gain a deeper understanding of their institutional context and (b) examine the impact diversity work was intended to have, and was having, on campus.

The guidelines recommend that the evaluation plan be organized around a central question—*how will we know we are making progress?*—and include the following components:

- **Project overview:** includes a description of current diversity efforts, institutional goals for diversity, strategies to achieve those goals, and the institutional enhancements anticipated as a result of the proposed goals;
- **Methods and instruments:** includes a discussion of how a campus will monitor progress on institutional goals and assess the effectiveness of particular strategies;
- **Process:** includes a description of how a campus will create and implement the evaluation plan and share evaluation results with a broad group of constituents.

The guidelines stress that the plan be self-contained, succinct, accessible to a variety of audiences, and designed so that constituents can track whether anticipated progress is actually occurring. The guidelines also provide a sample evaluation template to illustrate how a campus can chart goals, strategies associated with each goal, methods of measurement, information about data collection, the person(s) responsible, baselines, benchmarks, and timeframes by which to gauge progress. This type of visual display also allows leaders to quickly and easily share this information with constituents across campus.

An excerpt of the sample evaluation template is located on the following two pages. This excerpt depicts one goal (improving the retention and success of URM students) within a set of goals a campus would want to establish to undertake comprehensive diversity work. It also depicts one strategy (for this example, improving the advising system) out of a set of strategies that a campus would employ to make progress on each goal. As noted earlier, campus leaders would be wise to utilize a comprehensive framework for diversity, such as the one put forth by Smith (1995), to ensure that goals and related strategies span broad areas of institutional functioning.

Excerpt of Samp[le]

Goal/Intended outcome	Measures	Data collection, mechanisms, and instruments	Who will be responsible
Increase retention and success of URM students	GPAs of URM students Persistence toward graduation year by year Percent achieving honors	GPAs, institutional graduation data (4–6 yrs), and annual persistence by entering cohort Percent receiving honors	Registrar
	Quantitative information about URM students' in-class experiences, out-of-class interactions with faculty, and utilization of academic support resources	College Student Experiences Questionnaire™ survey items on academic engagement	Survey administrat[or]
	Academic advising notes on URM students' academic experiences	Sample of academic advising notes on URM students' experiences from across departments and class levels (e.g., freshman, sophomore, etc.)	Evaluation team le[ader] or member

St[rategies]

Strategy X	Measures	Data collection, mechanisms, and instruments	Who will be responsible
New advising effort	Student/faculty satisfaction with frequency of contact between advisers and students	Faculty and student advising surveys	Survey administrat[or]
	Student course-taking patterns Attrition from individual courses	Transcript review that tracks students' performance	Assigned adviser
	Student and faculty perceptions about the advising system	Focus groups/interviews with a sample of faculty and students	Evaluation team le[ader] or member

...aluation Template

Baseline (if applicable)	Benchmarks	Timeframe for review
...nt GPA and retention rates	URM student success rates mirror or exceed those of other groups	Annually
...l levels of engagement	URM student engagement mirrors or exceeds that of other groups	
...sers' initial note-taking patterns regarding URM ...ents' academic experiences	Advisers systematically and consistently collect detailed information about URM students' academic experiences	

...ies

Baseline (if applicable)	Benchmarks	Timeframe for review
...ulty and students' current views on advising	A 20 percent increase in student/faculty satisfaction with frequency of contact between advisers and students	Annually
...blish URM students' course enrollments at the ...inning of each term ...ertain the degree aspirations and/or intended ...ors of URM students	URM student retention in courses mirrors or exceeds that of other groups URM course-taking patterns are on target to lead them to their degree aspirations and/or intended major at levels that mirror other groups	At the conclusion of each term
...cument perceptions of the advising system the ...m prior to implementing new effort	Focus group/interview participants identify specific elements of the advising system that foster or inhibit URM student success and offer suggestions for improvement	Each term, with different samples of faculty and students

Appendix 4
Summary of *CDI Evaluation Project Resource Kit*

Full document available at: www.aacu.org/irvinediveval/pdfs/ResourceKit_11_05.pdf.

The resource kit is designed to help campuses create evaluation plans to measure outcomes related to their campus diversity initiatives. The kit includes instruments to measure eight major areas related to campus diversity (e.g., campus climate, student satisfaction, and intergroup relations), a list of selected Web sites related to diversity and evaluation, and a selected bibliography. The table of contents follows.

The resource kit will be especially helpful to campus leaders who seek to monitor progress in creating learning environments that (a) tap the educational benefits of a diverse community of faculty, staff, and students and (b) extend these benefits to everyone in that community. Users should note that the resource kit is not a pre-packaged design plan. Campus leaders would be wise to spend some time reviewing the introductory section—as well as pertinent references in the bibliography—to help define the type of evaluation design and plan that will fit their needs. They then may want to spend time with colleagues thinking through what it is they want to measure and how best it might be measured. Once these steps have been taken, it may be helpful to review the summary descriptions of the various tools and select a set to explore in more detail. Many of the tools are available online, which can greatly aid this process.

CDI Evaluation Project Resource Kit

Table of Contents

SECTION ONE

Institutional Framework for Monitoring Progress 4

SECTION TWO

Instruments 16
    Campus Climate.. 16
    Student Satisfaction 35
    Intergroup Relations 50
    Faculty Perceptions 57
    Student Learning and Involvement... 64
    Curriculum.. 73
    Alumni... 78
    Administration/Staff... 84

SECTION THREE

Miscellaneous Reports, Tools, and Frameworks......................... 92

SECTION FOUR

Evaluation Websites (selected) 103

SECTION FIVE

Bibliography (selected) 107
    Student Learning... 107
    Diversity... 109
    Organizational Learning... 112
    Appreciative Inquiry.. 117
    Institutional Change.. 124
    Evaluation and Assessment... 128

About the Authors

Alma R. Clayton-Pedersen is the vice president for education and institutional renewal at the Association of American Colleges and Universities. Clayton-Pedersen directs the Network for Academic Renewal and the Greater Expectations Institute and leads grant-funded work in college success with the Pathways to College Network, a consortium seeking to increase college access and success for underserved students. Prior to her time at AAC&U, Clayton-Pedersen spent more than fifteen years at Vanderbilt University where she served in a variety of roles, including associate dean for undergraduate academic affairs for Peabody College. While at Vanderbilt, Clayton-Pedersen conducted more than twenty studies for the division of student affairs, including a longitudinal study of freshman student withdrawal from the university, and, with colleagues, a campus-wide study of student interracial interaction as an indicator of the campus climate for diversity. She is a coauthor of *Enacting Diverse Learning Environments: Improving the Climate for Racial/Ethnic Diversity in Higher Education,* which provides a framework of the dimensions of campus climate and illustrates promising practices to enhance the climate for diversity.

Contact Alma Clayton-Pedersen at clayton-pedersen@aacu.org

Sharon Parker is a senior research associate at Claremont Graduate University, a resource faculty member at Evergreen State College in Olympia, Washington, where she resides, and a consultant on issues of diversity. Prior to serving with the CDI Evaluation Project, Parker served in a number of positions focusing on diversity, including president of the American Institute for Managing Diversity, a nonprofit organization dedicated to studying the relationship of diversity initiatives to organizational development; director of social responsibility programs for the Union Institute; and associate provost and director of multicultural development at Stanford University. Parker has also served as an evaluation consultant for various diversity initiatives, including those at several colleges and universities across the country, the five-year evaluation of the Compact for Faculty Diversity, and early projects related to AAC&U's American Commitments initiative.

Contact Sharon Parker at WorkinDiversity@aol.com.

Daryl G. Smith is professor of education/psychology in the school of educational studies at Claremont Graduate University. Prior to assuming her faculty role, Smith served as a campus administrator for twenty years in student affairs, planning, and institutional research. Her research and writing during the past seventeen years have focused on institutional approaches to diversity and in recent years on evaluation strategies related to diversity. In addition to numerous articles and papers, she is an author or coauthor of *Interrupting the Usual: Successful Strategies for Diversifying the Faculty, The Impending Loss of Talent: Challenging the Assumption of Testing and Merit,* and *Achieving Faculty Diversity: Debunking the Myths.* With five other evaluators of national diversity projects, she has also been a coauthor of *To Form a More Perfect Union, A Diversity Research Agenda,* and *Assessing Campus Diversity Initiatives,* published by AAC&U. She has worked with numerous foundations to develop evaluations for funded projects and has served as a consultant to many campuses.

Contact Daryl Smith at daryl.smith@cgu.edu.

José F. Moreno is assistant professor in the department of Chicano and Latino studies at California State University, Long Beach. His areas of emphasis are Latino/a education and policy studies, organizational learning, diversity and education, pre-college outreach programs, and evaluation methods. Previously, Moreno was an assistant professor and senior research analyst at the Claremont Graduate University school of educational studies and was senior institutional researcher at Pomona College, in addition to serving with the CDI Evaluation Project. Prior to that, he was a postdoctoral scholar in the division of education at the University of California, Davis, where he studied the long-term influences of pre-college outreach programs for the nationally recognized Puente Project. Moreno served as editor for *The Elusive Quest for Equality: 150 Years of Chicano/a Education* and coeditor for a special issue of the *Journal of Educational Policy* that focused on Puente.

Contact José Moreno at jmoreno7@csulb.edu.

Daniel Hiroyuki Teraguchi is dean for diversity and academic advancement at Wesleyan University. There he serves as a resource, advocate, and principal adviser on diversity issues to the campus community. Prior to joining Wesleyan, Teraguchi served as associate director of the office of diversity, equity, and global initiatives at the Association of American College and Universities, where he served as a conceptual and administrative leader in grant-funded initiatives that provide resources to colleges and universities working on comprehensive educational change.

Contact Daniel Teraguchi at dteraguchi@wesleyan.edu.